SpringerBriefs in Electrical and Computer Engineering

More information about this series at http://www.springer.com/series/10059

Dennis Anderson • Robert Wu
June-Suh Cho • Katja Schroeder

E-Government Strategy, ICT and Innovation for Citizen Engagement

Springer

Dennis Anderson
St. Francis College
New York, NY, USA

Robert Wu
St. Francis College
New York, NY, USA

June-Suh Cho
College of Business Administration
Hankuk University of Foreign Studies
Seoul, Korea (Republic of)

Katja Schroeder
St. Francis College
New York, NY, USA

ISSN 2191-8112 ISSN 2191-8120 (electronic)
SpringerBriefs in Electrical and Computer Engineering
ISBN 978-1-4939-3348-8 ISBN 978-1-4939-3350-1 (eBook)
DOI 10.1007/978-1-4939-3350-1

Library of Congress Control Number: 2015950837

Springer New York Heidelberg Dordrecht London

Printed on acid-free paper

Springer Science+Business Media LLC New York is part of Springer Science+Business Media (www.springer.com)

Preface

Since the first computers were introduced in the 1940s, information and communication technologies (ICTs) have transformed the world we live in. Governments have been the pioneers of this transformation from the beginning of the first electronic computer which changed humanity profoundly. In the private sector we have seen how ICTs were used to reach out to build relationships with customers and businesses. Twenty years ago, a pure online business or e-business was an aspiration. The concept of online shopping was still new in the mid-1990s and was considered as a fad or an added feature to the brick-and-mortar business. Today it is a norm or a de facto business model. The private sector has gone through a major transformation within a short time period.

While governments have followed the private sector in adopting technologies, until recently, there was no national strategic planning for ICT. In fact, many governments were slow to adopt technologies and remained largely paper-based. Some governments, like Sweden and Denmark, were more progressive. They adopted ICT earlier and set an example for others. Having a national strategy (or framework) on ICT in government and e-government can significantly reduce government waste, corruption, and inefficiencies while increasing transparency and accountability. Some governments have been opening up to citizens via e-government, and others are learning from successes and failures as they build their own e-government portal or infrastructure. Over the past decades, the United Nations Department of Economic and Social Affairs (DESA) through the Division for Public Administration and Development Management (DPADM) has provided support to current 193 member states for intergovernmental processes, comparative policy research and analysis, education and training, and advisory services related to e-government and e-governance.

This book discusses current trends and best practices in e-government and e-governance. It explores the three levels of e-government and national strategies that foster the achievement and realization of the tertiary level of e-government.

Those strategies include the development of a citizen-centric and participatory e-government and the leveraging of recent developments in social media technologies that have empowered citizens around the world to demand government reform and greater transparencies.

New York, NY, USA — Dennis Anderson
Seoul, South Korea — Robert Wu
New York, NY, USA — June-Suh Cho
Katja Schroeder

Acknowledgment

This project was truly a team effort. We would like to thank our research assistant, Peng Xu, M.S., for his diligent assistance on this project. Peng is currently pursuing his M.P.A. from the School of International and Public Affairs at Columbia University.

In addition, we would like to express our deep gratitude for the value guidance that Dr. Adriana Alberti has given us. Dr. Alberti is a global eminent e-government expert who has made tremendous contributions to e-government development for more than a decade.

Contents

About the Authors

Dr. Dennis Anderson, Ph.D., is chairman and professor of Management and Information Technology and the Institute of E-government and Sustainability at St. Francis College, New York City. He also serves as executive chairman of the Center for Entrepreneurship at St. Francis College. He is also an eminent global adviser and expert of e-government and public administration to the United Nations Expert Group. Anderson received his Ph.D. and M.Phil. in mathematics education from Columbia University. He also received an Ed.M. in instructional technology and media from Columbia University. In addition, Anderson holds an M.S. in computer science from New York University's Courant Institute of Mathematical Sciences and his B.A. in computer science from Fordham University. He also completed an executive-education program in e-commerce at Columbia University's School of Business and Harvard University's Institute for Management and Leadership in Education Program. For full bio, visit http://www.drdennisanderson.com.

Robert Wu, J.D./M.B.A., is assistant professor of accounting and business law and the director of the Center for Entrepreneurship at St. Francis College, New York City. He has held numerous accounting and legal positions within private, nonprofit, and government institutions including Big Four accounting firms, investment banks, and the US Department of Homeland Security, Immigration and Customs Enforcement, and the City of New York. He holds a B.S. in accounting, magna cum laude, from The University of Akron, an M.B.A. from Case Western Reserve University, and an M.S. from the University of Pennsylvania, and he earned his Juris Doctor from St. John's University School of Law. He is licensed to practice law in the State of New York and before the US Tax Court.

Dr. June-Suh Cho, Ph.D., is presently a professor of the College of Business Administration at Hankuk University of Foreign Studies in Korea. He also had conducted research at EC & Data Management group in IBM T.J. Watson Research Center. Dr. Cho's research focuses on electronic commerce, CRM, multimedia databases, e-government, and security. He has published articles in IEEE, ACM, and other conferences and journals. Dr. June-Suh Cho holds a B.A. from KyungHee University in Korea, an M.S. in computer science from New York University, and a Ph.D. degree from Rutgers University.

Katja Schroeder, M.A., is a global communications consultant and strategist. She has led award-winning communications campaigns for clients in North America, Europe, and Asia-Pacific. Her passion is to create a dialogue about how technology enables socioeconomic development. To help innovative companies gain market traction, Schroeder founded the PR agency Expedition PR. Schroeder holds both a master's in information and communication sciences from Sorbonne in Paris, France, and a master of arts in communication from Free University in Berlin, Germany. She is certified as a CSR practitioner (CSR-P) by the Centre for Sustainability and Excellence and the Institute of Environmental Management and Assessment (IEMA). Schroeder teaches marketing and PR at St. Francis College, Brooklyn, and sits on the board of the College's Center for Entrepreneurship.

Chapter 1
Introduction: Global Challenges in Turbulent Times: Road to Sustainable E-government

Our main task is to overcome the point at issue, our economic crisis. However, we also have to prepare for our future. Therefore, our full-scale promotion of informatization is valuable as a new growth engine for the future of Korea.

– Former President Lee Myung-Bak, the Republic of Korea

Governments around the world are exploring ways to better manage the challenges posed by population growth and climate change. The world will need to grow around 70 % more food to feed a population of nine billion people and is far from being perfect today (Rotman, 2013).

Natural catastrophies, political uprisings and socio-demographic changes will not make the tasks of creating better living conditions in the future any easier. We are caught up in a race between improving the human condition, using science and technology, and battling a series of financial, political and environmental crises.

The Millennium Project's Global State of the Future Index provides a score card on humanity's performance in addressing the most important challenges in 2011 (Table 1.1). With limited and diminishing resources, how can we meet all challenges? How can we prioritize them?

The complexity of these challenges illustrates that the issues are no longer localized. There must be cooperation at an international level, and partnership between citizens and governments, private and public sectors. The Great Recession has shown us that everything is interconnected and interwined. In an environment where the cycle of information is continuous, it has changed the way we work and live. For example, we bank and shop after hours. As global consumers, we are no longer limited by the constraints imposed by brick-and-mortar vendors. Despite all of the social, economic and environmental changes, we have an opportunity to change the way governments operate and interact. Information and communication technologies (ICTs) can help connect multiple parties to create a collaboration platform, achieve participation and solve problems.

The first electronic computer was invented in the 1940s (Mackintosh, 1988), but only a few people would recognize it as such. The first electronic computers had formidable stature given their enormous physical size. However, their limited

D. Anderson et al., *E-Government Strategy, ICT and Innovation for Citizen Engagement*, SpringerBriefs in Electrical and Computer Engineering,
DOI 10.1007/978-1-4939-3350-1_1

Table 1.1 The world score card by the Millennium Project

Where we are winning	
1.	Improved water source (% of population with access)
2.	Literacy rate, adult total (% of age 15 and above)
3.	School enrollment, secondary (% gross)
4.	Poverty headcount ratio at $1.25 a day (PPP) (% of population) (low- and mid-income countries)
5.	Population growth (annual report) (a drop is seen as good for some countries, bad for others)
6.	GDP per capita (constant 2000 US$)
7.	Physicians (per 1000 people) (surrogate for health care workers)
8.	Internet users (per 1000 people)
9.	Infant mortality (deaths per 1000 live births)
10.	Life expectancy at birth (years)
11.	Women in parliaments (% of all members)
12.	GDP per unit of energy use (constant 2000 PPP $ per kg of oil equivalent)
13.	Number of major armed conflicts (number of deaths >1000)
14.	Undernourishment (% of population)
15.	Prevalence of HIV (% of population 15–49)
16.	Countries having or thought to have plans for nuclear weapons (number)
17.	Total debt service (% of GNI) (low- and mid-income countries)
18.	R&D expenditures (% of natural budget)
Where we are losing	
19.	Carbon dioxide emissions (kt)
20.	Global surface temperature anomalies
21.	People voting in elections (% of population)
22.	Levels of corruption (15 largest countries)
23.	People killed or injured in terrorist attacks (number)
24.	Number of refugees (per 100,000 total population)
Where there is uncertainty	
25.	Unemployment, total (% of total labor force)
26.	Non-fossil-fuel consumption (% of total)
27.	Population in countries that are free (% of total global population)
28.	Forestland (% of all land area)

computational power, which is far less powerful than a smart watch, provided those machines with limited utility. A few decades later, it is almost impossible to imagine a world without computers. Even the founder of IBM, Thomas J. Watson Sr. could not imagine the transformational power of computers, predicting, "I think there is a world market for maybe five computers" (Anderson & Cho, 2010). The invention of computer networks, telecommunication technologies, and the Internet, has changed everything from manufacturing to news media to banking. Specifically, in the last two decades, personal and mobile computers, the Internet, and telecommunication technologies, collectively known as information and communication technologies (ICTs), have made this transformation possible. This first wave of the

Fig. 1.1 Electronic numerical integrator and computer (ENIAC), first-generation computer (U.S. Army photo)

Information Technology Revolution is similar to the first Industrial Revolution, in which the private sector has played the predominant role in accelerating change, i.e., from the brick-and-mortar traditional business model to the "click-and-mortar" e-business model. This necessary transformation was a painful experience for many. Initially it was greeted with cynicism and skeptism but within 15 years, it is impossible to imagine a world without e-businesses and we automatically expect to find an answer on the Internet instead of going to the local library. Even the stacks at libraries are undergoing changes and adopting a more virtual catalog of offerings. For these institutions, the writing on the wall is clear: adopt or perish (Fig. 1.1).

Even with all of these technological advancements, the public sector and governments have been lagging behind in adopting and taking advantage of the benefits (Hirschheim & Smithson, 1999; Irani, 2000; Irani & Love, 2001; Jones, Irani, & Sharif, 2007; Remenyi & Money, 2000; Willcocks & Lester, 1999). There is general acceptance that with the right strategy and application of ICTs, governments can be more efficient and provide better services to their citizens (U.N., 2013). This will also bring accountability to the government spending. This book will examine strategies for e-governments and how effective application of ICTs can improve government services for citizens and help achieve the optimal services and bring transparencies to the government business.

At the turn of a new century, in recognition of global poverty, the 192 United Nations member states agreed to eight global goals known as the Millennium Development Goals (MDGs) "which range from halving extreme poverty to halting the spread of HIV/AIDS and providing universal primary education, all by the target date of 2015."[1] The eight goals[2] include the following:

Goal 1 – Eradicate extreme poverty and hunger
Goal 2 – Achieve universal primary education
Goal 3 – Promote gender equality and empower women
Goal 4 – Reduce child mortality
Goal 5 – Improve maternal health
Goal 6 – Combat HIV/AIDS, malaria and other diseases
Goal 7 – Ensure environmental sustainability
Goal 8 – Develop a global partnership for development

In order to facilitate the achievement of the established MDGs, 18 targets were identified (The transformation of government, World Economic Forum, 2005). According to the 2009 MDG Progress Report, there has been some progress on some of the goals but most targets are either "progress insufficient to reach the target" or "no progress or deterioration" (MDG Annual Progress Report 2009, Statistics Division of the United Nations Department of Economic and Social Affairs). The UN Department of Social and Economic Affairs highlighted the following shortfalls which were based on the 2009 Annual Millennium Development Goals Report[3]:

- In Sub-Saharan Africa and Southern Asia, poverty remains stubbornly high. The number of '$1day poor' went up by 100 million in Sub-Saharan Africa during 1990–2005.
- The declining trend in the prevalence of hunger observed since 1990–1992, was reversed in 2008, largely due to reduced access to food because of high food prices and the global financial and economic crisis. The highest hunger prevalence in 2008 was in sub-Saharan Africa, where 29 % of the population was undernourished.
- 72 million children of primary school age around the world – about half in Sub-Saharan Africa – remain out of school.
- The rate of growth of CO_2 emissions has been much higher during 1995–2004 than during 1970–1994, and the trend has not changed so far.
- Gap in access to Internet between the developed and the developing world remains large. In 2007, there were only 13 users per 100 people in the developing regions, as compared to 64 in the developed regions. The digital divide also remains wide, both among and within countries. (The Millennium Development Goals: A Snapshot, UN Department of Economic and Social Affairs, 2010)

Since 2007, trillions of dollars worth of wealth was wiped out within 4 years. The world has gone through a number of crisis: housing, subprime credit, oil price, insurance, weak consumer confidence, unemployment, and sovereign debt (Isidore, 2011). The gap between haves and have-nots are widening even in developed

[1] http://www.un.org/millenniumgoals/bkgd.shtml

[2] Ibid.

[3] http://www.un.org/millenniumgoals/pdf/MDG_Report_2009_ENG.pdf

countries which sparked the Occupy Wall Street Movement (The World Bank, 2012). There is a global discontentment with governments from New York to New Delhi (Timmons, 2008).

A global effort to invest in the resources for key priorities is needed if the MDGs are to be achieved. This includes providing funding, expanding public-private sector partnerships, and investing in human resources, education and training, and ICTs. Governments, along with civil societies, NGOs, and educational institutions must collaborate in order to achieve these goals. Governments must be transparent, accountable, and accessible to curb corruption, ensure that resources reach the needy, serve citizens better, and create a smart and sustainable future.

The UN's post-2015 objective is to address all of the goals challenged in the framework of sustainable development, which was agreed upon by the UN Member States at *Rio + 20*, the UN's Conference on Sustainable Development during June 2012. It is a governmental imperative to create a sustainable and citizen-centric growth model and to emphasize that sustainable development consists of many elements, including healthcare, education, gender equability and social cohesion. Moreover, we should tap the potential of scientific knowledge, and technological advancement and innovation, and transform public governance to achieve our vision.[4]

ICTs have a critical role to play in this process. For example, a carefully planned resource management system can help deploy resources to a specific population in need of those resources, resolving problems in a targeted manner, instead of current models of resource distribution based on political interests (i.e., "pork barrel"). ICTs can help governments tackle system-wide corruption and facilitate reform towards more open, transparent, and accountable governments. Indeed, some of these changes are already taking place in the form of e-government.

1.1 What Is E-government?

E-government was popularized during the so-called "dot-com" era during the 1990s. The emergence of e-commerce and Y2K[5] ("doomsday") advanced e-government, as governments began to adopt the changes taking place in the private sector. E-government is defined in various ways (Relyea & Hogue, 2004; Seifert & Relyea, 2004). Some of the more antiquated definitions limit the scope of e-government as being merely a unit of a larger governmental entity (Gant et al. 2002). Other definitions of e-governance integrate its functions throughout the government.

World Bank defines e-government as "the use by government agencies of information technologies (such as Wide Area Networks, the Internet, and mobile

---

[4] H.E. Ambassador Nestor Osorio, United Nations Committee of Experts on Public Administration, 12th Session, April 2013.

[5] The total cost of Y2K was "revised to $1 trillion or more. Reuters reported Jeffery Boonmee, founder and president of Bicom Link, as saying Y2K is now a $3 trillion global industry, and that in the United States alone, the market for Y2K solutions is worth about $800 billion." (The True Cost of Y2K, Smart Computing, August 1999, Vol. 7, Issue 8).

computing) that have the ability to transform relations with citizens, businesses, and other arms of government." (Jeong & Kim, 2003; Kushchu & Kuscu, 2003; Trimi & Sheng, 2008) These technologies can serve a variety of different ends: better delivery of government services to citizens, improved interactions with business and industry, citizen empowerment through access to information, or more efficient government management (Gronlund & Horan, 2005; Reddick, 2005; Tian & Tianfield, 2003). The resulting benefits can be less corruption, increased transparency, greater convenience, revenue growth, and cost reductions. (Definition of E-government, World Bank[6]) E-government is a transformation of government processes, transactions, and policy making and implementation that are efficiently carried out through information and communication technologies to provide better and efficient services to the citizens while reducing waste and corruption and increasing accountability, transparency, and trust. Furthermore, it is about creating a one-to-one relationship with the government in which citizens are empowered to take part in the democratic process and policy making.

E-government is increasingly being implemented in all areas of government administration at both the local, regional and national levels, increasing efficiency and transparency and bringing convenience and safety to citizens' lives, and consequently improving the quality of life (Fountain, 2001; Mulgan, 2000; Northrup & Thorson, 2003). For example, there are growing numbers of initiatives promoting e-participation, e-governance and e-services: 70 % of the United Nations Member States in 2012 provided a consolidated one-stop-shop portal for public services compared with 26 % in 2003.[7]

While e-government was initially promoted as a means of improving internal management efficiency in public administration, e-government is increasingly considered an important measure for enhancing citizen access to government services and expediting the delivery of services to citizens (Morris & Moon, 2005; Streib & Navarro, 2006). It is used to enhance citizens' access to government as much as government's access to citizens using current network technologies (Irani, Love, & Montazemi, 2006; Premkumar, Ho, & Chakraborty, 2006; Heeks & Bailur, 2007; Seifter & Chung, 2008).

The seventh annual measurement of the progress of online public service delivery across Europe report mentions 20 common basic public services, including the following:

- Income taxes: declaration, notification of assessment
- Job search services by labor offices
- Social security benefits
- Personal documents: passport and driver's license
- Car registration (new, used, imported cars)
- Application for building permission
- Declaration to the police (e.g. in case of theft)

[6] http://go.worldbank.org/M1JHE0Z280, May 2012.

[7] United Nations e-Government Survey 2012

Fig. 1.2 Kiosks application in India

- Public libraries (availability of catalogues, search tools)
- Certificates (birth and marriage): request and delivery
- Enrollment in higher education/university
- Announcement of moving (change of address)
- Health related services (interactive advice on the availability of services in different hospitals; appointments for hospitals) (The Annual Report, 2007)[8]
- Government to Business transactions (licenses, permits)

Some of these services, like personal documents, licenses and certificates, are available to local people in developing countries like India using kiosks. (West Bengal Upgrading the State Machinery, CIO India) (Fig. 1.2).[9]

According to the United Nations e-government program, e-government "encompasses the capacity and the willingness of the public sector to deploy ICT for improving knowledge and information in the service of the citizen. Capacity espouses financial, infrastructural, human capital, regulatory, administrative and systemic capability of the state. The willingness, on part of the government, to provide information and knowledge for the empowerment of the citizen is a testament to the government's commitment." (United Nations E-Government Readiness Knowledge Base (UNKB)[10]) (Division for Public Administration and Development Management (DPADM), 2012) E-government is not simply a web-based or Internet government portal for citizens, nor it is simply ICT infrastructure or resources such

[8] The annual report "The User Challenge – Benchmarking The Supply of Online Public Services" prepared for the European Commission, Directorate General for Information Society and Media, September 2007.

[9] http://egovernance.wordpress.com/category/states-in-india/

[10] http://www.unpan.org/DPADM/MajorPublications/UNEGovernmentSurvey/EGovernmentReadinessKnowledgeBaseUNKB/tabid/718/Default.aspx

as Enterprise Resource Planning (ERP), mobile networks, and Business Intelligence (BI). The essence of e-government is embodied in the idea of forming a symbiotic relationship between the government and its citizens, and effectively using ICTs to facilitate that relationship while promoting transparencies so that the citizens can place greater trust in the activities of their governments. Over the past three decades, some countries, particularly developed countries, have gone through some transitions using ICTs along with the new understanding of the role of ICTs and clear goals and objectives. For the vast majority of governments, however, e-government is still at a conceptual level rather than an operational directive.[11]

1.2 E-governance

E-governance in its broadest sense can be thought of as "the continuous optimization of service delivery, constituency participation and governance by transforming internal and external relationships through technology...Government to Citizen, Government to Employee, Government to Business, and Government to Government" (Fang, 2002). E-governance, however, can be thought of more practically as the "how-to" part of implementing a more mobile government governance structure that provides the guidelines for managing processes and enforcing policies.

According to the latest corruption perception index published by Transparency International, general public distrust of government is widespread and those perceptions transcend borders.[12] The root of corruption is often the government that has no, or seriously lacks, effective governance and, in some cases, those governments even encourage and propagate systematic corruption. For example, a 2013 survey by PwC of global accounting and reporting by central governments around the world highlighted the lack of financial disclosure transparency in many central governments, and stressed the need for more robust systems of accounting and financial reporting.[13] What happened to billions dollars that went to underdeveloped countries? Despite apparent receipt of financial aid, many of them are going backwards and getting poorer. A cynical view would point out the subterfuge created by these ministers, and the lack of financial transparency is required because they do not want to share their budget and how they spend their budget. They would rather leave their budget items ambiguous. These governments have bad governance or no governance at all.

Kleptocracies have been entrenched into many of these countries that lack effective governance that are ostensibly in existence to promote the common welfare

[11] UN E-Government Survey 2014.

[12] See Transparency International's Corruption Perceptions Index 2014 (citing deep-seeded distrust of government in than two-thirds of all countries); Available: http://www.transparency.org/cpi2014/results#myAnchor1

[13] https://www.pwc.com/en_GX/gx/psrc/publications/assets/pwc-global--ipsas-survey-government-accounting-and-reporting-pdf.pdf

when, in reality, many are simply there to unjustly enrich the individual government agents from the treasure trove of national resources, like minerals, oil or gas.

Even in the United States, corruption exists in various forms by exploiting legal technicalities. Many times, the people who stand to benefit the most from these contracts and deals are the power brokers who do not necessarily want transparency. However, effective governance is a critical element to effective governance. Furthermore, in order to make e-governance effective and work for the citizens, whom should be the focus and intended beneficiaries of good governance, the government must have a clear policy on corruption and transparency, including providing more information online, simplifying administrative procedures, and streamlining bureaucratic functions. This can be as simple as having an e-mail address to contact the appropriate government office to address citizen concerns. It can be thought of similarly to a customer service e-mail contact on an e-commerce website. Without a customer service contact on a website, the efficacy of the online shopping could be called into question.

As of today, some 25 % of the 193 United Nations Member States have embarked on Open Government Data initiatives.[14] Governments are starting to publish data collected by public institutions and leading to greater transparency and value co-creation.

According to statistics gathered by various organizations, citizen trust in their governments has been diminishing in many parts of the world.[15] In some advanced democracies, including the United States and selected countries of Western Europe, voter turnouts are decreasing. Many view the growing influence of money in the electoral process and the strong role of special interests on public policy decision-making as being antithetical to the letter and spirit of democracy (Lessig, 2011). A similar trend is emerging in developing countries. A recent study by UNDP shows that in Latin America expectations and hopes for a better future, which followed the Third Wave of democratization, have slowly been replaced by apathy and distrust in government.[16] According to the aforementioned study, the inability of governments to deliver adequate services, especially in the social sphere, as well as to promote more employment opportunities and better living conditions for all, have resulted in a widespread disappointment among the population and the value of democracy per se is being questioned. Perhaps most critically, some democracies have not been able to address the question of equity and social justice effectively.

In the last quarter of a century, poverty and lack of opportunities is still a persistent challenge for many countries around the world. Capitalism may be a driver of some of these issues. Capitalism flourishes in democracy but it creates a less equitable society, and systemically widening the gap between "haves" and "have-nots".

---

[14] H.E. Ambassador Nestor Osorio, United Nations Committee of Experts on Public Administration, 12th Session, April 2013.

[15] The 2013 Corruption Perceptions Index (0–100) by Transparency International http://cpi.transparency.org/cpi2013/results/

[16] http://unpan1.un.org/intradoc/groups/public/documents/un/unpan024933.pdf

1.3 E-government Sustainability

E-government should not be seen as a project in itself. It should be looked at a macro level (government as a whole) as well as a micro level (units that make up the government). It is about connecting these micro units to create a functioning and sustainable e-government. In order to create a sustainable e-government, it requires to address the following three aspects that the United Nations identified as critical.

- Economic sustainability: how e-government supports efficiency and effectiveness in government for greater growth and development by employing whole-of-government approaches. Hierarchical and bureaucratic structures need to be transformed into horizontal integrated systems, which facilitate customer orientation and increase levels of transparency and accountability in a move towards public service delivery solutions that are sustainable.
- Social sustainability: social equity and inclusion are possible only if institutional barriers to citizen inclusion are removed and opportunities for their participation through ICTs are equitably distributed. The reach of innovative inclusive solutions to support citizen decision-making processes is just as important as the nature of the participatory process itself. For social sustainability, the role of e-government requires a shift from that of a controller of information and services to that of a facilitator, whereby information and services are geared towards addressing the needs and concerns of the citizenry, especially the vulnerable, and to promoting user uptake.
- Environmental sustainability: e-government can support environmental institutional integration by bringing environment agencies online and linking them with governance structures responsible for development planning so that coordinated solutions can be found that are efficient, effective, and sustainable.

Chapter 2
Effective, Inclusive and Citizen-Oriented Service Delivery, and Governance Innovation

If you can book dinner on Open Table, or a flight on Southwest or United online, then why shouldn't you be able to make an appointment at your local Social Security office the same way?

– President Barack Obama, USA

2.1 Effective, Inclusive and Citizen-Oriented Service Delivery

An effective public administration and inclusive government institutions, at the national, regional and local levels are, arguably, the most important factor in the successful implementation of a national development agenda. The State's fundamental functions, which include establishing a regime for protection of rights over person and property, providing for the common defense, promoting the general welfare, promoting social justice and otherwise ensuring law and order cannot be accomplished without effective governance and public administration institutions, human resources and other complementary processes.

The 2012 Report to the Secretary-General on the "Future We Want for All", has strongly highlighted that inclusive social development, environmental sustainability and inclusive economic development "depend, critically, on effective governance capacities at national, local and municipal levels, including political commitment and leadership; and on the legal and economic empowerment of people, especially those most excluded, and of their civil society organizations, to participate effectively in national and local decision-making. (…) Effective governance is also central to the systemic transformations of economies in ways that support rights-based, equitable and sustainable development." (page 31, 2012).[1]

Governance and public administration plays a central role in development since effective, inclusive and efficient service delivery is critical to addressing issues of poverty eradication and is at the heart of prosperous societies. The quality of, and access to, education, health, water, sanitation, justice, security, technology as well

[1] See UN System Task Team on the Post-2015 UN Development Agenda, "Realizing the Future We Want for All, Report to the Secretary-General", June 2012.

D. Anderson et al., *E-Government Strategy, ICT and Innovation for Citizen Engagement*, SpringerBriefs in Electrical and Computer Engineering,
DOI 10.1007/978-1-4939-3350-1_2

as the promotion of gender equality in service delivery, and provision of services for employment opportunities and private sector development (providing effective, low-cost and quality services to formalize property rights, open up a business, access financial services for low-income people and vulnerable groups, especially women, etc.) provides the essential tools for citizens to empower themselves to live a dignified life.

Global commitments to sustainable development and poverty reduction require that all citizens, men and women, have equal access to quality services. If governments lack the capacity to deliver or provide access to services, the attainment of the Millennium Development Goals (MDGs) and the Post-2015 UN development agenda is unlikely to be achieved. Much progress has been made in achieving the MDGs in many parts of the world, however, results remain inconsistent and there is a growing recognition that "business as usual" is not the answer to sustainable development.

Governments must achieve innovation in their systems, institutions and processes in order to achieve tangible results and have a positive impact on the lives of citizens. To overcome these challenges, governments need to devise and implement innovative strategies and practices that can allow them to do more with less; reach out more effectively to vulnerable groups; and engage citizens through innovative mechanisms in public policy-making decisions and service delivery. In times of multiple crises requiring a comprehensive governmental response, there needs to be innovation in the manner in which governments respond to multi-faceted challenges, thus adopting "whole-of-government" approaches.

Although government is still central to society, it is now widely recognized that governance is not the sole prerogative of governments, and therefore partnerships with civil society and the private sector and participation of all stakeholders is central to innovative public administration (Alberti & Klareskov, 2006). In sum, innovation in public governance is a contemporary necessity of every country that desires to find concrete and innovative solutions to a number of social and economic challenges, including poverty, unemployment, poor education systems, health epidemics (including HIV/AIDS and the avian influenza), gender discrimination, environmental degradation and the effects of climate change.

2.2 Innovation in Service Delivery Is Critical

As shown by the United Nations Public Service Awards[2] and a number of other award programmes in various regions of the world, there is great capacity in every region of the world to reinvent government and to launch innovative practices in service delivery. The global flow of ideas, practices and approaches between and within countries has assumed increased importance over time, thus the great

[2] The United Nations Public Service Awards is the most prestigious international recognition of excellence in public service.

importance of this Government Summit. Disseminating information, through the Government Summit, about innovations in government, and most importantly, transforming this information into knowledge so that it may benefit countries looking for effective solutions to governance problems, is an effective capacity-building activity.

There is no "silver bullet" solution to the myriad complex issues facing countries. However, sharing information and transferring knowledge on innovations are important tools for stimulating and inspiring governments in their reform efforts toward more inclusive development. In fact, learning from other countries' experiences in reinventing government through knowledge exchange can save time and inspire new reforms. Why re-invent the wheel? In some cases, it can help countries leapfrog various stages of development.

Innovation in public governance has many definitions, and there exists a rich literature on the subject matter. Generally, innovation can be defined as a creative idea which is implemented to solve a pressing problem of public concern (Van de Ven, 1986). In short, it can lead to a solution to a governance challenge. It is the act of conceiving and implementing a new way of achieving a result and/or performing work. Innovation can refer to new products, new policies and programs, new approaches, and new processes.[3] It can involve:

- The incorporation of new elements,
- A new combination of existing elements, or
- A significant change or departure from the traditional way of doing things.

It is important to bear in mind that innovation is not an end in itself, but rather an instrument to improve services for the benefit of all. As the economist Schumpeter, once stated: "Innovation is mankind's effort to endlessly pursue change for a better world" (Schumpeter).

2.3 UN Public Service Awards: Service Delivery

According to the (UN Public Service Awards, 2013), there are four main principles that should guide innovation efforts in service delivery as follows:

- **Quality** – High quality service delivery may be manifested in – but is not limited to – the availability of government services at times and in ways that are more convenient to the public, speedy processing of applications or claims, reduction in the amount of paperwork and other activities citizens must perform in order to demonstrate compliance of clearly written government regulations.
- **Access** – such as the expansion of the coverage or enhancement of quality service delivery to vulnerable groups is critical to inclusive social development.

[3] See "Innovation in Public Governance: Replicating What Works", 2006, United Nations.

- **Cost-effectiveness** – Utilizing the most economic models for delivering quality services to the citizens and ensuring effective delivery is essential, particularly in times of financial crisis (ICT Compendium, 2007).
- **Citizen-centric** – Utilizing mechanisms that have proven to collect feed-back from citizens and that succeed in engaging them in the delivery of services.

Progress in increasing the quality, access, cost-effectiveness and responsiveness of public services has been uneven across the globe. While some countries have been able to successfully reform their public service delivery systems and institutions to meet today's challenges, others have not been able to do so despite several efforts. Based on the review of innovative practices from around the world, particularly those initiatives that have won the United Nations Public Service Awards, and building on the lessons learned, there are five critical enabling factors to promoting innovation in service delivery:

1. Shared visionary and committed leadership
2. Collaborative institutional frameworks
3. Culture of innovation
4. Engaging citizens and building partnerships
5. Utilizing ICTs

2.4 Strategies for Innovation in Service Delivery: A Holistic Approach

According to several UNPAN reports, in several countries, the delivery of services has not been effective and responsive to the needs of citizens in general because of (a) weak leadership and human resources capacity, i.e. leaders are unable to elaborate a shared vision articulated in a clear policy framework, as well as to promote strategic and participatory planning, implementation, monitoring and evaluation of service delivery; (b) weak horizontal and vertical institutional arrangements to allow for integration of services and seamless service delivery; (c) lack of public administration processes and mechanisms that allow for the participation of citizens in the definition of priority areas, allocation of funds, as well as design and delivery of services, (d) lack of an organizational culture that promotes innovation through knowledge sharing and management, as well as increased transparency and accountability for increased efficiency, effectiveness and responsiveness of service delivery; and (e) weak national ICT infrastructure; low usage due to inadequate e-literacy and low utilization of ICTs to deliver services.

In order for governments to provide key public services in an equitable, effective, inclusive and citizen-centric way, the capacity of the public sector to deliver services must be strengthened at national and local levels. This implies strengthening four major and inter-twined dimensions of the public sector, namely the institutions, particularly at the local level, to deliver services; the leadership and human resources capacities needed to deliver services in a transparent, equitable, efficient and accountable manner; the processes and mechanisms that favour the participation of citizens in the design and delivery of services; and the organizational culture so that it may provide a fertile ground for continuous improvement and innovation in service delivery.

Based on a review of innovative cases, there are five central strategies to promote innovation in service delivery as follows.

1. Innovative transformation of leadership and public officials' capacities
2. Institutional and organizational innovation
3. Process innovation, including innovative channels and mechanisms for partnership building and citizen engagement
4. Organizational culture to promotes knowledge sharing and management for innovation, transparency and accountability
5. Leveraging the potential of ICTs: new opportunities for innovation

These five strategies are inter-linked and inter-dependent and therefore should be considered in a holistic way. In other words, it is essential to address in an integrated and holistic manner strengthening institutional frameworks, processes and mechanisms to deliver services equitably and effectively, human resources capacity-building for equitable service delivery and ICT development and utilization.

2.4.1 Innovative Transformation of Leadership and Public Officials' Capacities

Strategic leadership is a critical ingredient of innovation. Improvements are made when leaders are able to mobilize stakeholders in the design and implementation of service delivery. It implies that the quality of human resource management has a significant impact on the performance of government institutions.[4] Studies have shown that the quality of human resource management has a significant impact on the performance of government institutions.

> A United Nations University (UNU) recent study which examined the relationship between the capacity of state bureaucracies and poverty reduction ... concluded that there is indeed a strong relationship between states with competent and effective public institutions and their ability to reduce poverty.[5]

Strengthening leadership capacities at both national and local levels is a prerequisite for creating an environment where innovation thrives. It is important that government officials, particularly at local level, have the appropriate attitudes, skills and expertise to harness ideas from diverse communities for innovation and to

[4] See United Nations Department of Economic and Social Affairs: Unlocking the Human Potential for Public Sector Performance: World Public Sector Report 2005: (United Nations, New York, www.unpan.org), p. 26, para. 1.

[5] Ibid.

engage citizens through new channels and modalities. Local governments must embrace innovation by necessity because of their proximity to the people whom they serve.

Among the challenges requiring visionary leadership (especially at local level) are those triggered by the growing demands for inclusive participation and good governance, and for the accommodation of ethnic, cultural, gender, political, economic, and religious diversity. Leaders cannot design and implement strategies on their own, nor is it desirable for them to do so. Leaders that are not particularly aware of and sensitive to issues of diversity will not only miss the opportunities provided by the socio-cultural and even politico-economic diversity, but they will also fail to pay particular attention to creatively mediate the demands that are created by this diversity.

Embracing and harnessing diversity for development starts with acknowledging the unique roles played by society's constituents. Experience over time has shown that no matter how much one wants to help local communities to develop, the task is by far easier when the communities participate in that development process (Kauzya, 2010). Those communities can get involved in planning, programming, prioritising, implementing, monitoring and evaluation of their development. This new type of interaction between public officials and citizens requires new skills, attitudes and knowledge, as well as the capacity to utilize effectively social media and other ICT tools.

Public servants can effectively deliver desired services in a timely manner, when they behave transparently and ethically, demonstrate accountability and integrity, and are responsive to the needs of the people and mirror the diversity within the population. Being responsive requires governments to go beyond the usual rhetoric and uncover citizens' needs as increasingly, the citizens' realities count and are crucial in the design and implementation of public programs.

Shaping, or re-shaping values, attitudes and behaviors in the public sector through the elaboration of codes of conduct containing guiding principles, which can include the following as a culture of service: excellence and quality, responsiveness, efficiency, etc. Representative public officials should take part in the redefinition of their codes of conduct to enhance ownership as well as alignment of behaviors and values. In promoting human resources development in an innovative public sector, particular attention should be given to:

- Diversity management and gender responsive service delivery
- Knowledge management
- Horizontal management
- Resource and information management
- Partnerships and negotiation skills
- Communication and ICT skills

As institutional and structural arrangements of the public service can only be operationalised by human beings, there is strong need to enhance the ability of individuals to perform responsibilities effectively and to realize their potential. Although training is the basic engine for capacity expansion, it needs to be supplemented by other capacity building activities. Knowledge, skills, values and attitudes of staff at all levels need to be re-adjusted to match the functions, responsibilities, and tasks along with the new work methods.

Internal and external individual aspects are strongly inter-related as much as the internal and visible collective aspects are also inter-linked, whatever the situation. Nevertheless, more often than not, great attention is focused on changing the visible collective structures of governance institutions without paying too much attention to the realignment and, at times, the leverage of the internal/invisible side of governance institutions. The main concept here is that values and mindsets have a direct impact on behaviour, relationships, partnerships, as well as on culture, stories/myths, and vice-versa, which affect institutions, organizations, policies and infrastructure. All of these elements must be aligned for successful innovation in service delivery. Changing only the visible structure of governance systems and institutions without a transformation of the related values and attitudes will not produce the expected results.

In sum, the following points can be highlighted:

- Strategic leadership capacity-building is an important tool to foster innovations in governance.
- Experience has shown that strategic leaders encourage responsible risk-taking and are open to ideas from members of the team.
- The type of leadership also affects the sustainability of an innovation.
- If an innovation is based on a leader and it is not institutionalized, the innovation will die as soon as there is a change in leadership.
- Public managers need to align three key pillars: public value, organizational capacity, and legitimacy.

2.4.2 Institutional and Organizational Innovation

Governance and leadership capacity cannot be expanded in the absence of a nurturing institutional infrastructure. With public sectors offering an increased number of services, the focus is shifting from what kinds of services are provided to how they are provided. Many countries provide a host of services, and those services are increasingly coordinated and customized to better fit the needs of the citizens. More often service delivery operations are integrated early in the value chain or services bundled in a single entry point for the citizens. For example, in the Philippines, gender and development mainstreaming efforts led to the creation of the Davao Medical Center, which, in turn, set up the Women and Children Protection Unit (WCPU) – a one-stop family crisis intervention centre, which provides legal, psychiatric and medical services to its patients. In Brazil, the Bahia's Citizen Assistance Service Centers (SAC) bring together federal, state, and municipal agencies in a single location, convenient to the public such as shopping malls and major public transportation hubs, to offer multiple government services. There are many other valuable practices of client-focused, one-stop service delivery for social services and mobile service delivery for multi-service clients in remote areas.

Integrating services requires a reorganization of institutional frameworks, processes, accountability mechanisms and work modalities through "whole-of-government" approaches, which allow for integration. Traditionally, governments have operated in the context of highly specialized and compartmentalized institutions, often times working in "silos". Whereas in the past, a fixed division of labour among ministries and departments was essential to the consolidation of an effective bureaucratic system based on the Weberian model, in the twenty-first century such strict division no longer seems to fit the needs of more complex societies. In fact, low degrees of communication and coordination across agencies have led, in many instances, to redundancies and waste of resources. This ultimately results in poor service delivery and an inability to effectively tackle multi-dimensional challenges for economic growth, social progress and environmental protection.

A number of factors increasingly require governments to integrate and coordinate policies and decision-making processes for service delivery. Promoting effective collaboration among government agencies across all levels of government (national and sub-national) and with non-governmental actors is due to: (a) the growing complexity and interconnectedness of present development challenges, such as poverty eradication, environmental sustainability, disaster prevention and crisis management, which require integrated and holistic responses and services that integrate and address cross-cutting areas; (b) an increase in citizens' expectations for effective, equitable and citizen-centric services (including security, education, health, justice, shelter, sanitation, etc.), which entail a shift from an inward, disjointed and process oriented approach to a results based citizen-centric approach, requiring coordination, collaboration and integration of processes and services for reduction of red tape and improved service delivery; and (c) increased citizens' demands for meaningful participation in public consultation and decision-making processes, which call for innovative governance and collaborative mechanisms that allow citizens to actively take part in decisions that affect their lives and in service delivery.

As a result, several governments across the world are adopting whole-of-government or collaborative approaches through the promotion of horizontal and/or vertical initiatives, greatly aided by modern technologies, which provide useful tools to enable collaboration across agencies. While each agency continues to be accountable for its defined and focused role, cross-agency issues are addressed in a coordinated manner through new institutional and accountability frameworks and mechanisms. Greater communication and coordination among policy areas and agencies at all levels, are helping governments deliver "as one" in pursuit of increased quality of and inclusive access to services to the benefit of its citizens.

The model aims at centralizing the entry point of service delivery to a single portal where citizens can access all government-supplied services, regardless of which government authority provides them. In some countries, the whole-of-government approach helps build a transparent government system with interconnected departments and divisions, feeding into the funnel of greater government efficiency and effectiveness. Reviewing options for public service delivery, including decision-making processes, different delivery options and balancing fiscal sustainability and other policy challenges; preparing public sector budgets and making choices about prioritising public expenditure to make best use of limited resources in difficult times.

Integrated and coordinated service delivery at the national level and among the national and local levels, requires:

1. Policy coherence, legal and regulatory frameworks
2. HRM capacity development
3. Improved knowledge management and communication
4. Reorganization of finance and budget to address complex challenges
5. Mobilizing and connecting partners and stakeholders
6. New coordination and accountability mechanisms and lines of responsibility with new coordinating bodies
7. Effective utilization of ICTs for seamless service delivery
8. Infrastructure, environment and technology

2.4.3 Process Innovation

2.4.3.1 Reaching out to Vulnerable Groups: Multi-Channel Service Delivery

Process innovation focuses on the improvement of quality of public service delivery and entails new ways of designing processes to ensure services are inclusive and accessible by all groups in society, including vulnerable groups, and that mechanisms exist to incorporate citizens' feed-back and involvement.

Citizens have diverse needs and demands for services; therefore it is no longer sustainable for governments to utilize one preferred way of service provision over the other. It is now ever more essential that governments exploit all possible delivery channels in order to reach out to as many people as possible, no matter how poor, illiterate or isolated. The increasing power of ICTs has also provided governments with the flexibility of providing services and information to citizens through multi-channels. The 2012 E-government Survey shows that 71 Member States partner with third party organizations such as those in the civil society or the private sector to provide e-services.

A 2012 survey by Accenture concluded that if government services are offered online, most people would use them.[6] Research in China also shows that digital and traditional channels supplement each other, particularly among vulnerable populations in rural areas (Fu & Xiao, 2012). One study also show that the phone remains an effective channel for solving problems whereas websites are more effective for getting information (Reddick & Turner, 2012). Therefore, governments must provide

[6] https://www.accenture.com/t20150703T035243__w__/sg-en/_acnmedia/Accenture/Conversion-Assets/DotCom/Documents/Global/PDF/Industries_14/Accenture-Digital-Citizen-Full-Survey.pdf

multiple channels for their constituents, allowing them a choice of conducting their business online, over the counter, over the phone, at a kiosk, or via mobile phone. It is, however, in the government's interest to move from over the counter to online services as it improves efficiency and also offers enormous potential for cost savings. According to a 2009 PwC report, the UK government would save between GBP 3.30 and GBP 12 per transaction by moving transactions online.[7]

As with so many other trends (e.g., digital divide, usage), mobile services and their consumption are increasingly important in this area, particularly in developing countries. According to the ITU, in 2011, 90 % of the world population has access to 2G mobile networks and 45 % to 3G networks,[8] making it an attractive option for communication especially because of its general affordability.

From simple SMS-based services in poor rural areas to smart-phones and web-based access in urban centers and developed countries, mobility is increasingly a desired and frequently used channels of communication across the world. From a measurement perspective, this can begin by identifying WAP websites, such as the one in Canada. Further, offline channels can be measured online by identifying whether websites provide information on how to conduct services via other channels. Highlighted 2 years ago, the Australian portal remains a best practice in this area as the homepage itself offers the "Government Shopfront Locator" which allows users to identify local government services by postal code, area, or type of service. The search feature comes with addresses, open hours as well as an advanced map to find them. As if that was not enough, the "Contact Government" feature on the homepage also offers the following services: telephone hotlines, contact your local member, departments & agencies and government online directories. But just as features offline should be able to be found online, the reverse is true as well. In Sweden, almost all government agencies are now in the habit of printing their website URL on their forms, giving constituents another channel through which to submit them. "While mobility is clearly dominating the topic at the moment, trends in multi-channel services delivery include digital-by-default in the UK, meaning that services are primarily being delivered digitally, and the extension of online channels, such as conducting services on websites external to the government, including from the private sector such as Facebook."[9]

2.4.3.2 Innovative Channels and Mechanisms for Partnerships and Citizen Engagement

There is a diminished belief that governments can solve problems on their own. Citizens can and should be part of the solution. Given the opportunity to actively participate in service delivery, citizens can contribute distinctive resources

---

[7] http://www.parliamentandinternet.org.uk/uploads/Final_report.pdf

[8] https://www.itu.int/ITU-D/ict/facts/2011/material/ICTFactsFigures2011.pdf

[9] http://undesadspd.org/CommissionforSocialDevelopment/Sessions/2013/EGMempowerment.aspx

Fig. 2.1 Australian national government portal: Government Shopfront Locator

(time, effort, ideas, expertise) and can keep public officials accountable. Moreover, citizens who depend on public services have strong motivation to contribute to their design and implementation, however, appropriate institutional mechanisms are needed to adequately channel citizens' views, opinions and to involve them in the design and delivery of services (Fig. 2.1).

They must also be effective in so far as they must be able to achieve concrete public results in an equitable way with limited resources. However, leaders cannot design and implement strategies on their own, nor is it desirable that they do so. It is increasingly being recognized that governance is more than government, and that civil society and the private sector are not just "customers" of public services or stakeholders, but that they can be and should be agents of change who can actively be part of the solution by working with their governments to solve local and national challenges. In other words, there is a strong paradigm shift in the role that civil society and the private sector can play in contributing to good governance.

Whereas in the past citizens were seen as passive receivers of services and governments were the main providers of "solutions", today in all corners of the globe we witness a shift in how services are being conceptualized, managed and delivered. Where citizens are involved in public decision- making processes and in public service delivery, there is an increased sense of ownership and greater sustainability of public initiatives, as well as more creative ideas on how to do more with less. Furthermore, leadership is not confined to the government level. In fact, there are many examples of public leaders who operate within civil society and the private sector and work with governments to find suitable solutions to their problems. Experience has shown that governments that made progress in promoting transparency and accountability, and in providing equitable and effective service delivery have developed innovative ideas and practices, making use, whenever possible, of information and communication technology, and relying on strategic partnerships. Participatory leadership and innovation in addressing problems of public concern are increasingly emerging as the key factors in creating a better life for all.

Bringing services and public officials closer to people (e.g., from national to regional level) often brings a higher level of inclusion, responsiveness and customization – and thus increased satisfaction on behalf of citizens and businesses. Based on a review of the UNPSA winning initiatives and practices from around the world (UNPSA, 2005), there are different levels of citizen participation in service delivery, co-production being the highest level of citizen engagement. Citizens can be informed of a service; can be consulted about specific aspects of a services; can be asked to take part in the decisions about the type of services needed by the community; and can be empowered to take part in the delivery of services. The different levels of citizen engagement in service delivery include: information, consultation, involvement, collaboration and empowerment.

Empowerment of people is at the root of economic and social development. It is becoming one of the core elements that underpins efforts towards the achievement of the three core goals of the World Summit for Social Development, including poverty eradication, full and productive employment and decent work for all, and social integration. As such, empowerment is a means towards the end of social development. All members of society should have the opportunity and be able to exercise the right and responsibility to take an active part in the affairs of the community in which they live.

Empowerment requires the full participation of people in the formulation, implementation and evaluation of decisions determining the functioning and well-being of our societies. It refers to the capacity of individuals or groups to autonomously foster the relationships and institutional interactions necessary for their well-being and productivity. This aspect of people's empowerment is closely linked to social integration and poverty eradication. It builds people's capabilities to participate. Ultimately empowerment is about the removal of social, political, legal and economic barriers to the active participation of certain social groups in society (U.N., 2012).

Of particular relevance is the importance of mainstreaming gender in service delivery. Gender-responsive public services, such as providing for skilled health personnel to attend to births, have indeed lagged behind national and international commitments on gender equality. Public authorities have a crucial role in ensuring that the service delivery needs of women are met as the latter represent the majority of those who access and use public services. Hence, there is a need to institutionalize gender-responsive public service delivery, and promote the exchange of good practices concerning inclusion of women and their needs in governance and public administration in order to contribute to social and economic development.

The worldwide spread of the internet and ICTs has massively expanded opportunities for the creation and promulgation of information. Greater knowledge sharing will be critical to induce the social transformative changes needed to achieve social empowerment. With the goal of empowering poor and marginalized women and men, social and economic development is a process of transforming institutions for greater inclusion, cohesion and accountability.

2.4.3.3 From Centralized Service Delivery to Decentralized Service Delivery

One of the most effective institutional arrangements to allow citizens to effectively take part in decision-making processes as well as in the design, implementation, monitoring and evaluation of the efficient and responsible manner of service delivery is through a decentralized form of governance.

Decentralized governance offers the opportunity to involve the immediate beneficiaries in the allocation of public funds and to use resources to suit local needs and priorities. In principle, decentralization facilitates greater participation of communities in problem analysis and the implementation of formulated solutions. In fact, lack of inclusiveness will reduce chances for governments to be effective at best, or providing services that do not address the needs of the local communities at worst. The loss of finite resources, citizen disenfranchisement and tarnished government image result from an unresponsive system of government. Inclusive and decentralized government is not merely concerned with meeting people's needs. Rather, it is about creating an environment in which people can address their needs.

Governments cannot afford to second guess their communities' needs. Decentralization promotes high-impact resource delivery through increased and more direct mechanisms of accountability. It also increases ownership and sustainability by allowing all groups in society to take part in the decision-making processes. Decentralization enhances the "voice" of citizens in designing, planning and monitoring service delivery through increased participation.

In many countries that have decentralized, most of the areas in which the MDGs and their targets have been set are mandates of local governments. For example, primary education, primary health care, sanitation and access to potable water are all targeted goals. Thus, it is critical that the search for solutions on increasing institutional and leadership capacity focus on both national and local levels of governance.

Recent innovative decentralized governance approaches have included decentralized policy development, implementation and evaluation, as well as decentralized budgeting and expenditure management assessments. In Morocco, for example, the PAGER project brings water to the rural population, taking advantage of the devolvement of operation and maintenance of water facilities to local communities. So far, the PAGER project has succeeded to increase the share of the rural population with access to drinking water from 14 % in 1994 to 60 % at the end of 2004.[10]

[10] African Development Bank Drinking Water Supply and Sanitation Project Appraisal Report, May 2006 (available: http://www.afdb.org/fileadmin/uploads/afdb/Documents/Project-and-Operations/Morocco_-_Ninth_Drinking_Water_Supply_and_Sanitation_Project_-_Appraisal_Report.pdf).

Apart from the benefits of clean water and adequate sanitation, PAGER has also had a substantial collateral impact on primary school enrollment in rural areas, with the attendance of girls surging from 30 % to 51 % because traditionally young children, especially girls, are charged with supplying families with water.[11]

In another example, also in Morocco, the establishment of regional facilities for controlling fresh exports of fruit and vegetable had a significant impact on the competitiveness of the sector.[12] It has changed the previous practice when businesses incurred prohibitive costs to compete in the international markets because of high expenses and rejection rates of products which were required to be transported to a small number of centralized facilities far away from the source of processing.

In Indonesia, in the Tanah Datar district in West Sumatra, decentralization of the school system, carried out in 2001, resulted in increased quality of teaching and improved condition of students from poor families. Key elements of innovation were limiting the number of students in each class, creating a reward-system for high performing students and teachers and instituting a performance-based contracting of headmasters.[13]

A harsh reality remains, however, since service delivery systems are not equitable because decentralization reforms in many countries are limited in scope and they do not ensure a real transfer of authority from the center to the periphery (Thede, 2009). The main challenge is how to ensure that governments have the capacity to facilitate participation at all levels. As authority is devolved to the local level, local capacity enhances and opportunities are generated to cultivate creativity and inventiveness. Overall, weak decentralized governance hinders quality and access to basic services.

The increasing power of ICTs has opened up a vast window of opportunities for new channels and modalities of participation in government service delivery. Some examples include 3-1-1 service from the City of New York and Boston's CitizenConnect.

Public-private partnerships are becoming essential national frameworks to facilitate greater public participation so as to achieve better utilization of resources and increased efficiency in service delivery. Strengthening the capacity of the State for social development and enhancing partnerships between the State and civil society is one of the central challenges of our times. Countries which have given priority to education, health, sanitation and building social capital are also those that have prospered the most economically. They have been able to integrate more rapidly in the global economy thereby enhancing the quality of life of its citizens. Civil society participation in identifying the social needs of local communities and citizens' involvement in the elaboration and implementation of social programmes have proven instrumental in this respect.

---

[11] Ibid.

[12] See USAID Partnerships at http://iipdigital.usembassy.gov/st/english/texttrans/2003/04/20030404164051ennoccmk0.1897852.html#axzz3gM3PmEQ4.

[13] For further information on this case, see: http://www.innovations.harvard.edu/

2.4.4 *Culture of Innovation, including Through Knowledge Sharing and Management for Innovation, Transparency and Accountability*

If governments are to achieve improvement in service delivery to the citizens, then there must be a paradigmatic shift in organizational culture. The new mindset should emphasize prospective outcomes rather than retrospective obstacles. It should involve thinking about possibilities rather than the barriers encountered in tackling specific problems. World leaders should recognize that inter- and intra-disciplinary sharing of knowledge is essential to creating the individual and organizational knowledge necessary for achieving an integrated approach to sustainable development. Greater knowledge sharing will be critical for transformative changes. As highlighted the Report to the U.N. Secretary-General, "limited knowledge hampers progress towards inclusive growth and employment creation, and technological progress for sustainable development."[14]

2.4.4.1 Knowledge Sharing Management Strategies

Sharing information and transferring knowledge about inclusive practices in public service delivery is one of the most critical government capacity development tools as it provides public sector institutions with an array of concrete solutions to complex governance challenges. Sharing knowledge about inclusive practices is also a powerful tool in promoting positive change as it provides a fertile environment for replicating and adoption of good practices. Therefore, a multifacted and holistic knowledge management strategy is essential.

Part and parcel of a holistic knowledge sharing management strategy is access to information and freedom of expression, which are critical elements for citizen participation in service delivery. Access to information requires increased transparency, which is crucial also for improved and more effective service delivery. In fact, one of the obstacles in providing basic services is corruption, which needs to be addressed by enhancing transparency and accountability in public service delivery in order to ensure that government funds are used to improve people's quality of life (Bertot et al. 2010). The need to ferret out corruption and efficient service delivery are inextricably intertwined. Moreover, corruption has a disparate effect of harm to the poor by diverting funds intended for development, undermining a government's ability to provide basic services, thus feeding inequality and injustice and discouraging foreign aid and investment. By adopting the new paradigm of "open government", governments can restore citizens' trust in public institutions making them more accountable and transparent, and ultimately helping reduce corruption.

---

[14] Report to the U.N. Secretary-General "Realizing the Future We Want for All" (available: http://www.un.org/millenniumgoals/pdf/Post_2015_UNTTreport.pdf).

> The ability of people to hold institutions accountable – for delivery of quality services; for responsiveness, recourse and transparency; and for setting and adjusting priorities and targets – is key to people's empowerment. Well-defined, rule-of-law-based performance standards and benchmarks for accountability can generate confidence among the public in their institutions, thereby building support for the global development agenda. Pluralistic, independent media may help raise public awareness about development issues, empowering people with information to better monitor implementation and performance and hold governments accountable. National measures of progress should be complemented with disaggregated data and qualitative information for better understanding of factors contributing to and impeding progress in improving peoples' lives.[15]

A culture of innovation through knowledge management and sharing, increased transparency and accountability lies at the heart of promoting innovative services, which requires:

1. Effective and integrated knowledge management systems utilizing ICTs.
2. Human resources capacity-building in information management.
3. Improved transparency and accountability.
4. Open data (providing government data so that it can be re-used by citizens who then create improved services).
5. Knowledge networks at different levels within and among countries.
6. Establishment of Awards programmes at different levels to collect, analyse and share good practices.
7. Open communication among all stakeholders.
8. Media and marketing campaign to raise awareness about services and ways to participate.
9. Structured exchange of knowledge on innovative practices within and among Countries.

2.4.5 *Leveraging the Potential of ICTs: New Opportunities for Innovation in Service Delivery*

The global spread of the Internet and the application of ICTs in government, as well as greater investments in telecommunication infrastructure coupled together with capacity-building in human capital, can provide formidable opportunities to transform public administration into an instrument of development that is responsive to the needs of its citizens. ICTs are powerful tools for social and economic development. It promotes people's empowerment, participation, access to information, education and networking possibilities for all social groups, particularly marginalized subgroups within the mainstream population (Bertot et al. 2010). ICT applications are introduced to upgrade service delivery, including in terms of their greater effectiveness, efficiency, timeliness and quality, for wider access to services, and a more "citizen-centered" approach to services.

[15] Report to the U.N. Secretary-General "Realizing the Future We Want for All" (available: http://www.un.org/millenniumgoals/pdf/Post_2015_UNTTreport.pdf).

The European e-government vision for 2010 "... points at the role of e-government as an enabler for better government, an intrinsic political objective encompassing a series of democratic, economic, social, environment and governance objectives. These objectives can be articulated around two major axes: pursuing cost-effectiveness and efficiency, and the creation of public value..." (European Commission, 2007).

Broadband[16] access increasingly emerges as a key enabler of economic growth, distance education and improved medical treatment of people in remote areas where advanced health care is scarce. Many Governments make broadband access a high priority item on their policy agenda. The Republic of Korea perceives pervasive broadband as a critical tool to increase industrial efficiency, create e-business and jobs, improve global competitiveness, and increase significantly per capita GDP (Frieden, 2005). Internet-based service has also a strong potential for enhancing transparency and democracy into many practices of public administration (Bertot et al. 2010). For example, evidence shows that the application of ICT in local government operations by establishing electronic public information offices, has enabled local policy makers and public officials to better interact with the public and individual citizens (Dawes, 2008). New Internet-based facilities allow citizens to better express their needs, participate in and influence policy-making, comment on policy implementation, provide feedback on government services and file complaints. This, in turn, leads to better government responsiveness and relevance of public service delivery (Dawes, 2008).

As information and communications technology is facilitating the flow of information between governments and the public, it is essential to work towards improved access to information and communications technology, especially broadband networks and services, and bridge the digital divide.

[16]"Broadband refers to telecommunications in which band of frequencies is available to transmit information. As a result more information can be transmitted in a given amount of time" (UN World Public Sector Report 2003, page 4).

Chapter 3
The Changing Role of ICT in Government: Lessons Learned

The Government recognizes the need for public services to be delivered faster, better and more efficiently to citizens and businesses. Intelligent, targeted use of information and communications technology (ICT) and e-government are key enablers for these improvements,

– Minister Brendan Howlin, Ministry Public Expenditure and Reform of Ireland

3.1 From Efficiency to Transformation

The role of ICTs has dramatically changed over the past decade (Dawes, 2008). Even in the private sector, until the mid-1990s, ICTs were commonly considered as corporate expenses or overheads with limited return on investments (ROIs). For example, the common notion was that any data center built by a corporation would quickly depreciate in value, as servers would quickly have to be upgraded or replaced which were expensive compared to manual processes. Today, it is unimaginable to think any business could operate effectively without computers. However, businesses managed their affairs without them for centuries and having computers that were very expensive and not powerful in businesses was a major commitment.

Governments had more passive approaches to adopting ICTs, often lagging behind the private sector (Liu & Yuan, 2015). There was also typically lack of a legislative framework for e-government, largely due to ignorance or unwillingness to adopt transparency and accountability and the cost. Many global organizations, including the United Nations, define e-government in transitional terms as stages or phases (The Report for Congress, 2003).[1] This implies that e-government is an evolutionary progress (Fig. 3.1).

However, as we have seen in the private sector, with new ICTs, it is not always necessary to go through the same stages that others have gone through. For example, even as it is too costly for some regions to install traditional telephone networks,

[1] United Nations Global E-Government Readiness Report, 2005 mentions five stages, p. 16; The Report for Congress "A Primer on E-Government", 2003 mentions four stages.

D. Anderson et al., *E-Government Strategy, ICT and Innovation for Citizen Engagement*, SpringerBriefs in Electrical and Computer Engineering,
DOI 10.1007/978-1-4939-3350-1_3

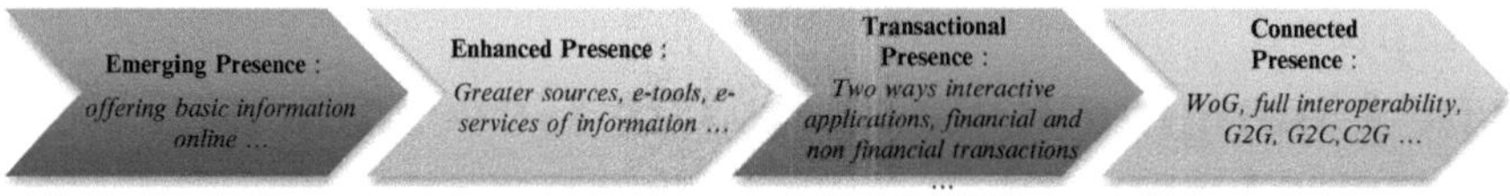

Fig. 3.1 The four stages of online service development, UNDESA

wireless telephone networks are often easier to install and less expensive, while helping to promote new businesses. With the new technologies, you can skip a generation or two also known as leapfrogging (The Economist, 2008). The explosion of mobile phones in Africa and Southeast Asia is a good example where "the penetration of the mobile phone is far greater than that of the Internet, especially in rural areas, making it the most accessible communication tool, according to Jon Gossier, founder and president of Appfrica, a technology company with headquarters in Uganda." (In Rural Africa, A Fertile Market for Mobile Phones, New York Times[2]).

Integrating newfound and local uses of ICTs, for example, mobile phones in TB clinics in South Africa and the incorporation of mobile currency (i.e., M-PESA in Kenya) in parts of Africa into e-government can be challenging, as different rules govern the market or community. Yet these challenges are accompanied by opportunities for government to enhance services to promote the local economy (i.e., microbanking). "Stephen Yeo, chief executive of the Centre for Economic Policy Research, said mobile phones had enabled developing countries to "leapfrog" old technologies." (Mobile growth fastest in Africa, BBC[3]) This idea of leapfrogging old technologies and using readily available technologies (or COTS – commercial, off-the-shelf) is very important to consider in e-government. Sometimes, they can offer a less expensive but effective solution. For example, many corporations are considering cloud computing (i.e., software as a service) which may offer a cost-effective option for their enterprise. Some of these approaches have a cost benefit but it is important to address security and privacy of the stakeholders as many of these services provide highly sensitive data (Fig. 3.2).

3.2 Changing Roles of E-government

3.2.1 From Information to Empowerment

In either transitional or transformational mode, there are three levels of e-government.

Level 1: Government-centric e-government – Government ICT represents a collection of disjointed massive data processing centers. Some characteristics

---

[2] http://www.nytimes.com/2009/10/06/science/06uganda.html?_r=1&scp=1&sq=mobile%20phone%20in%20africa&st=cse

[3] http://news.bbc.co.uk/2/hi/business/4331863.stm

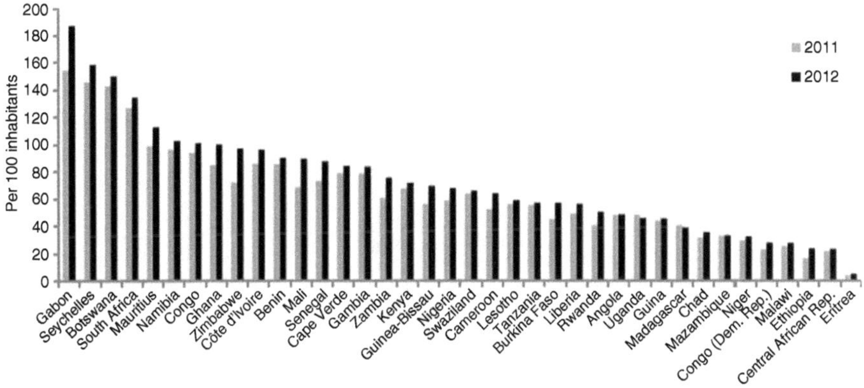

Fig. 3.2 Mobile-cellular telephone subscriptions per 100 inhabitants, Africa, 2011 and 2012, ITU world telecommunication/ICT indicators database

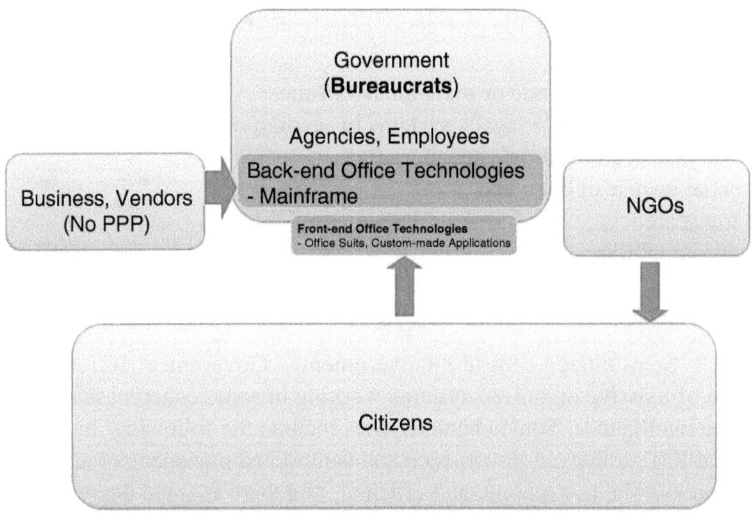

Fig. 3.3 Level 1, the role of ICT in government

include the following: uni-directional relationship with citizens where the government collects data from the citizens but no services are provided based on the data, or the government only selectively provides data to its citizens (i.e., informational web portal about public health); no national ICT strategy and governance; fractured ICT management; disconnected or broken business processes; disconnected, redundant and inefficient legacy systems; and no clear idea about the system inventory (Fig. 3.3). It is prone to corruption. There is no public-private partnership. Some negative aspects include the following:

- The overall system is too expensive;
- Too many local homegrown and legacy systems;

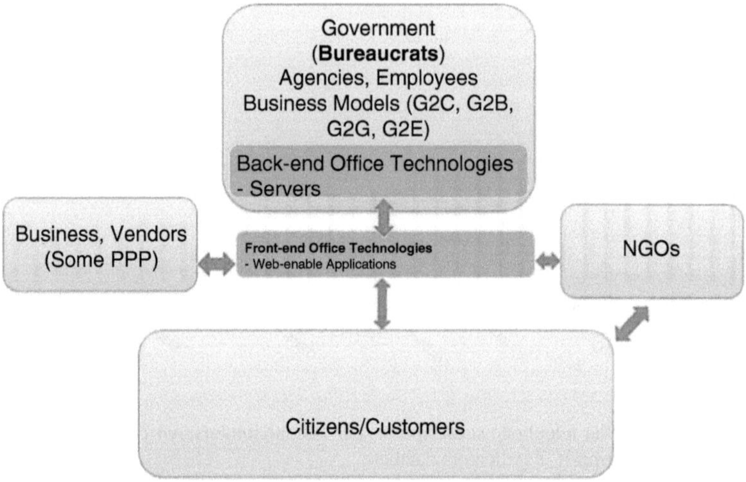

Fig. 3.4 Level 2, the role of ICT in government, e-government

- Too expensive to upgrade or maintain over time;
- Too many incompatible legacy systems to accommodate;
- No real data security or privacy measures;
- Potential misuse of data; and
- No transparency;
- No accountability;
- No business intelligence to support decision making; and
- No tangible economic benefit from the ICT.

Level 2: Semi citizen-centric e-Government – Government ICT represents a collection of massive organized systems working in some coherent manner to provide some intelligence. Some characteristics include the following: limited degree of national ICT strategy, e-governance and centralized management are somewhat reliable, accessible, transparent, and efficient, and there is some degree of connection between jurisdictions of governments (i.e., federal and local governments) and inter-agencies. Additionally, ICTs at this stage are considered an enabler, however, ICTs in most cases remains disconnected and redundant. ICTs are somewhat bi-directional at this level in terms of the government's relationship to its citizens, and it is more citizen centric (Velsen, Geest, Hedde, & Derks, 2009) (Fig. 3.4). Overall, ICTs are about cost-effective delivery of government services to citizens but, at this level, it is still not fully connected or integrated.

Today, many developed countries are taking advantage of new technologies like Web 2.0. tools (i.e., blogs, wikis, Twitter and Facebook, Instagram) and cloud computing (i.e., software as a service). There is also recognition that ICTs can improve or enable the government and its relationship with citizens (Davison et al. 2005). As it happened with e-commerce when it emerged, e-government is still considered as a subset or subunit of governments but this distinction is changing rather fast. It is about providing government services in cost-effective ways by integrating and improving business processes through ICT. In this environment, ICT can help facilitate transparencies and accountability by consolidating information and providing better intelligence about government processes and where the weaknesses or wastes are. There is a limit to what government can do and the private sector can play a vital role in building a win-win public-private partnership that could benefit both parties (i.e., building a high-speed broadband network) which could stimulate private sector growth and bring more revenue to the government. Some negative aspects include the following.

- Some upfront cost or investment is higher as many new ICT projects require more investment in the beginning (i.e., ERP implementation) (Kim et al. 2007).
- As new systems come into the government, there is higher demand for education and training.
- Hiring qualified personnel is challenging unless the government offers a competitive salary.
- Weak on data security and privacy (i.e., government employees can easily download sensitive data to an USB drive).
- Still much of the government system is disjointed and has duplicate systems with unknown amount of errors or inaccuracies.
- There is no clear understanding of what new applications will impact government businesses (i.e., Web 2.0. tools).
- There is no real ICT governance to mandate transparency and accountability. It is largely implied.

Level 3: Full citizen participatory e-government – Government ICTs represents a fully integrated and seamless e-system for all government functions (i.e., taxation, procurements, social services, health benefits, etc.) and it engages citizens to take an active role in the system (i.e., e-election and e-democracy). This participatory system cannot be realized unless it deals with contemporary issues including the following: security (cyber warfare), privacy, control, and most importantly trust (Davison et al. 2005). E-government is no longer distinguished from government as it is the one and same, made up of massive business intelligence processing centers and fully integrated, connected, consolidated, multi-directional, and efficient on-demand systems. It offers greater public-private partnerships as the government is open to continually improving its business processes to provide better services to citizens by reducing waste and increasing service performance. It could stimulate economic growth as it could empower entrepreneurs by providing tools that they need, instead of setting up obstacles. It also promotes accountability and transparencies within the government. At this level e-government is a fully sustainable model that can have a lasting impact on the country's resources and it can better manage its environment (air and water quality, carbon footprint, forest, transportation, etc.).

Some negative aspects include the following:

- Too much concentration of power within the government.
- Higher security and privacy risk.
- Delicate balance of personal freedom and the power of the state (Fig. 3.5).

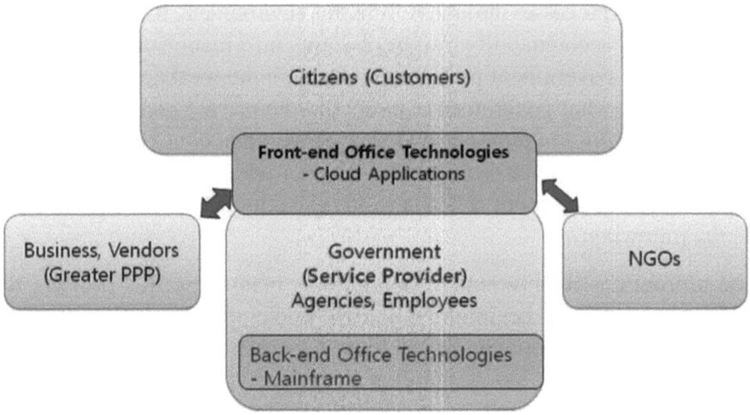

Fig. 3.5 Level 3, e-government and beyond

Fig. 3.6 Global PPP

Public-Private Partnership (PPP) could be a part of e-government success as governments cannot do everything (health, education, information access, etc.) due to the lack of resources, knowledge, or both (Jamali, 2004). The goal of PPP is not pure profit gain, so it is different from the typical vendor. PPP is about community interest (i.e., health, education, infrastructure) that could potentially benefit the government and private sector partner which involves all stakeholders working in concert (Fig. 3.6). For example, creating a nationwide high-speed broadband could benefit everyone. Citizens will have faster access, government will pay less for the network, private sector partners will be able to create services to make profit over time. PPP is new to many governments and having the right balance of profit sharing among these players is a major challenge. How to create a win-win ecosystem for all partners while stamping out corruption is very difficult even in governments with legal frameworks to deal with such issues. In order to have a transparent and accountable PPP, there must be an oversight body that includes citizen organizations to ensure there is no conflict of interest.

3.3 From E-government to M-government

The changing ICT environment and the increased use of smart phones have prompted some governments to explore new strategies with the mobile Internet services. This emergence of the mobile environment due to the fast spread of smart phones, tablet PCs, and other mobile devices has enabled the development of more intelligent and smarter services through convergence with other technologies (Fig. 3.7).

The strategic importance of mobile technologies is becoming more evident, as the wireless and mobile technology explosion increasingly affects the ways in which both governments and private enterprises go about their respective tasks. "Enabled mobility" offers new opportunities to provide more responsive public services through mobile applications and solutions (Song, 2005). The adoption of mobile government to support and enhance government performance and a more connected society is now inevitable. These revolutionary technologies allow citizens unprecedented access to their governments and services.

With this emergency of the IT-driven paradigm shift, mobile communication has become a part of everyday life. With strong demand for multi-channel service delivery, mobile technology leads naturally to an exploration of the potential utility and feasibility of m-government. In Canada, for instance, the government is processing a project called "Government of Canada Wireless Portal" to enable citizen access to government information using mobile devices. This service includes the contact information of members of Parliament, border wait time, economic indicators, passport services, and Canadian government news releases, etc.

As another example, Sweden, as a leading country of mobile technology, provides m-government services throughout the country. Services include SMS applications for city job postings, a mobile parking payment system, government inspector service, mobile healthcare providers, and a wireless map system called MapMate (Ostberg, 2003). Since 2007, the Seoul Metropolitan Government has introduced ⓜSeoul702, a mobile portal service through which citizens can suggest ideas and opinions about city policies (Cho & Soon, 2010) (Fig. 3.8).

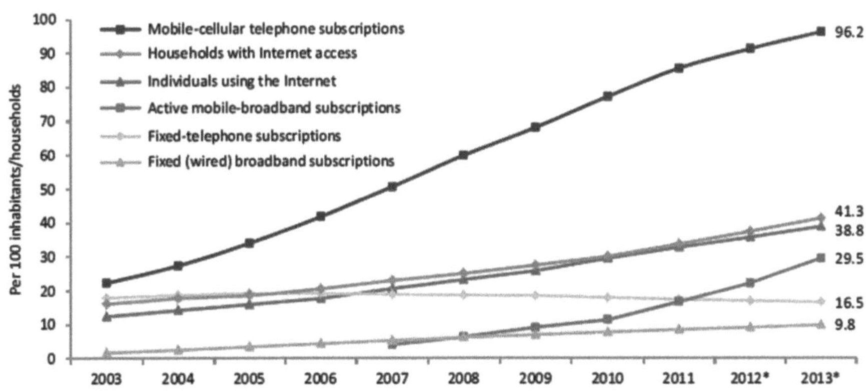

Fig. 3.7 Global ICT developments, 2001–2013, IT world telecommunication/ICT indicators database

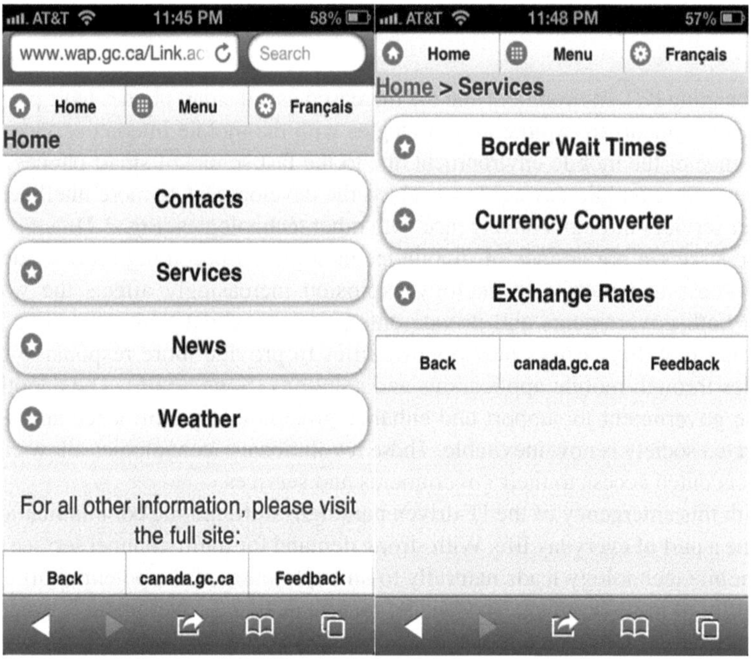

Fig. 3.8 Government of Canada wireless portal

M-Government is emerging as the next big wave for information and communication technology (ICT) use in the public sector. M-Government services, optimized by smart phones and other mobile devices, allow citizens and businesses to take advantage of the Internet to access government services, resulting in better perception and higher participation.

Growing research demonstrates the potential of mobile communications to radically transform government, provide access in areas where infrastructure required, but absent, for Internet or wired phone service, and where satellite phone is prohibitively expensive (Trimi & Sheng, 2008). As such, mobile government can help improve social and economic conditions in the world and it can play an important role in supporting the achievement of the MDGs and post-MDGs.

There are some fundamental differences between e-government and m-government service delivery. E-government involves the providing information electronically to geographically diverse, but technologically homogenous, ICTs. In contrast, m-government involves interactions in which the contexts of use are unknown. Accessing government services might be one of several activities being undertaken. Additionally, in m-government, the physical constraints of interacting with mobile devices limit the amount and type of information that might be located and accessed (Trimi & Sheng, 2008).

There are also challenges brought up by appearance of m-government. One of the most important questions with respect to developing technology for m-government is:

Table 3.1 TO-BE model for mobile government

	AS-IS	TO-BE
Device	Based on PCs	Smart phone, smart pad, etc. based on mobile devices
Infra	Internet based on the wire	Internet based on the mobile
Service	Based on PC	Seamless mobile services
User	Users for PC	Users for smart phone, etc.
Time & place	Constraint of time and space	Anytime, anyplace
Feature	One-way	Two-way

will e-government as we know it now be replaced by m-government as the dominant mode, or will m-government be just another access channel to public administration?

In light of the developments around the interaction between mobile administrations, mobile citizens, and mobile public officials, there is no doubt that the transition from e-government to m-government is not only a matter of a shift in the ICT technologies that are applied, but a more fundamental change. Such a fundamental change may lead to a different relationship between the mobile state and the mobile citizen, and between the mobile state and the mobile public official, as well as the growth of a different relationship between the citizen and the public official.

With the emergence of the IT-driven paradigm shift, mobile communication has become a part of everyday life. With strong demand for multi-channel service delivery, mobile technology leads naturally to an exploration of the potential utility and feasibility of m-government. The "Government of Canada Wireless Portal" serves as an example of m-government in action. Sweden and Seoul, South Korea are also taking charge of the m-government revolution as they seek to adapt their operations to a more mobile society.

Some primary direction of m-government include the following

- Citizens can use anytime, anywhere spread of mobile government services.
- Dynamic communication with citizens utilizing SNS.
- The mobile business practices without the constraints of time and space (Table 3.1).

3.3.1 Case Study of South Korean M-government

After going through continuous efforts in e-government and national informatization, South Korea has become one of the global e-government leaders. The South Korean government targets to become the world's best mobile e-government by delivering key e-government services that are representative of the most needed services by the public. And it will do so on a mobile platform. Furthermore, the have provided for the future direction of e-government as follows (OECD/International Telecommunication Union, 2011):

- The World's Best Mobile Government – They will transform the current internet-based government services, infrastructure and business environment into mobile-based services, and built service frameworks that are appropriate for the mobile environment. Identification of public services that can take advantage of the mobile, location-based, and real-time features of mobile devices, and establish bases for creating value-added services through the provision of private access to public information etc.
- Safe and Secure Public Life – They will establish fast and efficient counteraction systems against missing children, crimes, and disasters, using CCTVs and sensors etc. To improve public life, they will establish advanced alarm networks based on tracing of agricultural, livestock and fisheries products, and disease management through linkages with hospitals, using barcodes and RFID chips etc.
- 'Smart Work' – To achieving work and life balance, they will establish a 'smart work' environment and expand to private sector through the establishment of mobile offices in the public sector, identifying tasks adaptable to smart work, and improving personnel management systems.
- Personalized public service delivery based on communication – Expansion of public participation in policy making processes through including social network services (SNS) provides extended communication channels between government and the public through real-time access to public information. They provide the provision of customized services to the public and firms through integrated and one-stop delivery of information related to tax, public fees etc., and online one-stop processing of complex regulatory issues related to business activities .
- Solid and sound infrastructure for e-government – They provide the mandatory web standardization to support easy access to e-Government services to all corners of the society, including the marginalized members of our society. They are also trying to improve efficiency in use of information resources through the establishment of 'cloud computer centers' in the National Computing and Information Agency (NCIA), and strengthen security policies envisaged in the new mobile environment through prevention of theft or loss of smart phones, infection of malicious codes, and hacking.

3.3.2 Implementation Plan of Korean M-government

With increased demand for smart phone–based services, most government agencies are promoting competitive mobile services. In 2011, the Ministry of Public Administration and Security has established a roadmap, which is "Implementing smart government to establish ISP for mobile services' business through a public and administrative services".

Also, the government has established a common base mobile, mobile services and building guidelines, legal framework and governance system.

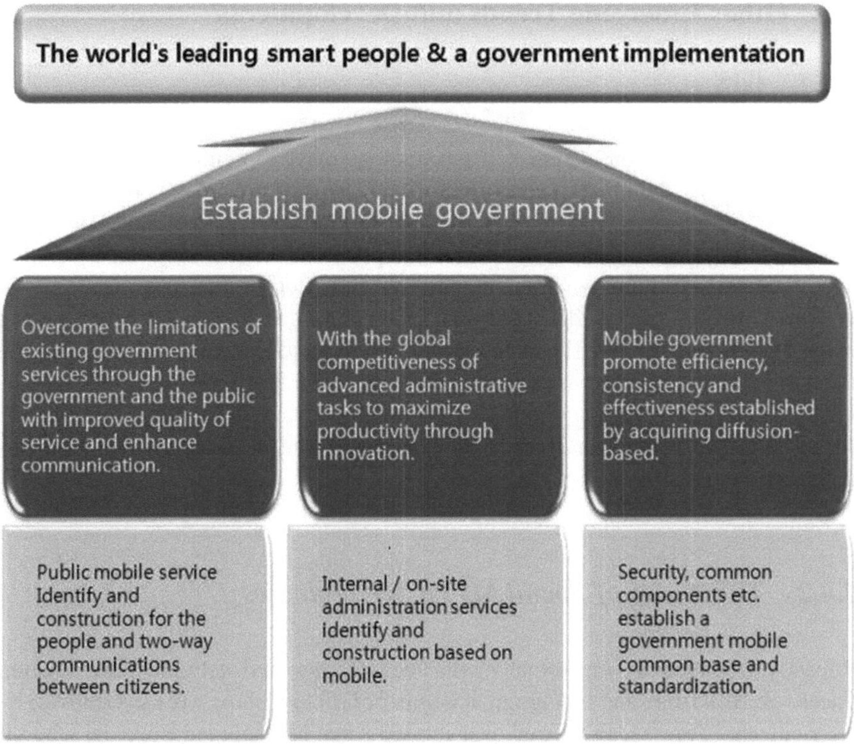

Fig. 3.9 The worlds' leading smart people & a government implementation of Korea

The implementation plan will be prepared for by preparing budgets at all levels by ensuring that agencies take advantage of factors, such as to prevent overlapping investment plans.

By 2011, general public administration to build mobile government services that can be used for guidance, is planning to propose guidelines, scheduled to provide guidelines are as follows:

- List of instructions and guidelines
- Mobile Government Services Management Guidelines
- Interface guidelines for mobile service's users
- Guidelines for mobile service deployment of the public administration
- Mobile service deployment guidelines for the people
- Common guidelines for mobile government services
- Security Guidelines for Mobile e-government services
- Mobile government services, utilizing standard framework guidelines
- Government utilizing social media guidelines (Fig. 3.9)

3.4 Other Emerging Trends and Developments

3.4.1 GIS

Geographic information system (GIS) technology played a central role in determining and checking the Internet access speed and status of broadband connectivity in different communities and neighborhoods. The technology not only produced broadband coverage maps; it also became a platform for fostering understanding and participation among government, citizens, and affected industries.

New York has utilized GIS in building and examining a broadband coverage map using a predictive model. The state reached out to local governments, encouraging them to validate data used to create the maps. New York also involved telecommunications and cable companies-that are sometimes wary of broadband initiatives for competitive reasons-and asked them to verify the information the state was collecting (Fig. 3.10).

3.4.2 The Power of Social Media Technologies

Recently, powered by the social media technologies and networks like Twitter, Facebook, YouTube, and Instagram, a number of dictatorships were overthrown by their citizens. This "Arab Spring" was ignited when Mohammed Bouazizi who set

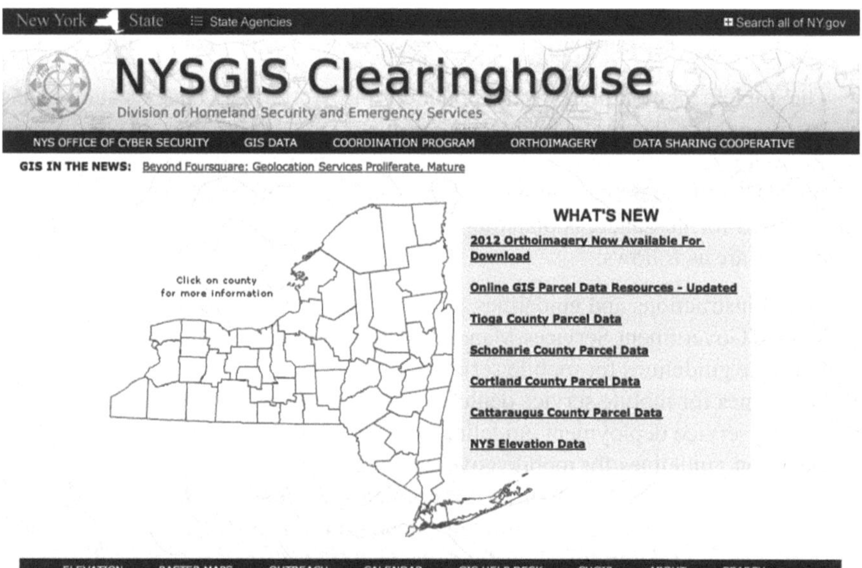

Fig. 3.10 NY state geographic information system (GIS)

himself on fire in protest of corrupted government died and a successful coordination of demonstrations led to the regime change (Ardıç, 2012). This soon spread to the region and later toppled Hosni Mubarak, the long time Egyptian dictator. Many developing countries like Egypt have a high number of youth and a very high unemployment rate among those youths (Ardıç, 2012). These two things have pushed the Arab Spring forward. They are simply not happy with the same old regime's status quo without much future. These young people are tech savvy and they have found new tools like mobile phones, social networks, and social media technologies to challenge and in some cases change the governments.

Dictatorial regimes should be on notice that citizens who can coordinate and unite will, and they can, change their governments. Heretofore, citizens never were possessed of those powers. In the past, the government can shut down the satellite or TV or radio station to have a total media block out while killing its citizens. However, today's social media technologies have changed the game. For example, Wikileaks.org has released thousands of dirty dealings and corrupt activities by various governments. Lack of government transparency essentially created the demand for sites such as Wikileaks.org, and only a fundamental change in government practices might stymie the demand for that brand of information.

3.4.3 Protection of Personal Information

The United States Congress enacted The Privacy Act of 1974,[4] which found *the right to privacy is a personal and fundamental right protected by the Constitution of the United States*. The United States Supreme Court doubled-down and reasserted the right to privacy in its jurisprudence through two subsequent cases: *Whalen v. Roe*[5] and *Nixon v. Administrator of General Services*.[6] The need for information privacy encompasses all segments of the population. However, citizens today are affected by government data collection and dissemination, and a number of privacy laws apply directly to this sector.

In recent years, many countries have introduced the e-government system. Government officials claim that e-government should boost efficiency because it would minimize the need to use documents. In fact, they are building a massive database covering the most intimate personal information belonging to the general public. Unfortunately, proper legislative systems are not in place yet for governing such collection of personal information. In the use of personal information by e-government, privacy protection is an area that requires attentive consideration (Dawes, 2008).

[4] Codified at 5 U.S.C. § 552a et seq.

[5] 429 U.S. 589 (1977).

[6] 433 U.S. 425 (1977).

The development of a proper e-government regulatory infrastructure is another essential element for the promulgation of e-government services. This will involve creating the foundation for trust in e-government by protecting the privacy of personal information.

Trust in e-government is an important precondition for service expansion. By enhancing the protection of privacy and security of information, citizens are assured that they can use e-government services safely. A privacy protection system of e-government is concentrating on prevention mechanisms, such as the analysis and establishment of potential privacy risks during the planning phases of an ICT project.

Furthermore, objective indices to measure the level of privacy protection activities of public agencies and improve protective measures will be developed and distributed. In addition, analysis and consulting for privacy protection activities of public agencies will be strengthened.

3.4.4 Public Services Through u-Service

The next step of e-government is to enable people to participate and communicate with the government by providing them with free and easy access to public services at any place and at any time, and with any device available. This is achievable through the convergence and integration of advanced information technology and government services.

Korea's "u-Service" strives to achieve a happy and safe society through promoting an IT Convergence Service (safety, welfare, infrastructure, environment, administration, and tourism) for citizens' personal lives. This is done by spreading u-Technology across the nation, and combining u-Service with u-Technology (e.g., RFID/USN, 3G mobile communication technology, Telematics, GPS, Augmented Reality and Cloud Computing).

Areas with the greatest potential impact for the industrial sector, such as logistics and distribution, agriculture, defense, and the environment are main targets for expanding and implementing services to stimulate the private sector.

u-Service with the smart convergence of IT is starting to open up a ubiquitous society providing reliable information and services anywhere, anytime, and for anything. u-Service leads us into a happy and safe society enabling various IT services anywhere in the nation. u-Service also has improved both efficiency and transparency of public services.

As the 'Smart IT' environment is expected to upgrade the citizen's overall lifestyles, working methods, and the social culture of the public, there has risen the need for the government to prepare application measures.

Korean government endeavors to provide a diverse u-Service by applying smart devices to both the public and private sectors. The plan for the Promotion of

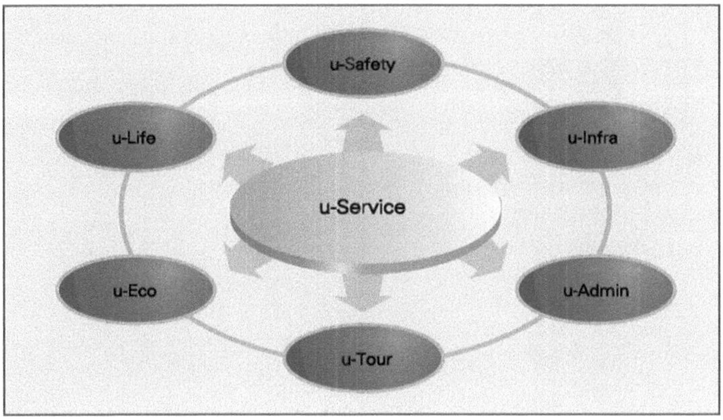

Fig. 3.11 Key areas of u-Service

Ubiquitous-based Public Services was established in March 2009 to provide the basis for expanding u-Technology across all sectors of society and the nation. Initial services were carried out in key six areas (u-Safety, u-Life, u-Infra, u-Eco, u-Admin, and u-Tour) with a strong relevance to daily lives and the projects have been identified with the objective of developing successful service business models (Fig. 3.11).

Chapter 4
Six Good Practice Case Studies

4.1 Critical Role of Local Governments in National E-government Development: Connecting the Dots

Local e-governments provide citizens with opportunities to understand broad policy issues by facilitating active discussions and encouraging participation in public administration. By inviting citizens to voice their opinions on policy issues and ultimately have these opinions reflected in the city's policymaking process, e-government can contribute to the production of better policies for citizens. Services for citizen customers are based on satisfying the diverse demands of individual citizens and incorporating citizens' opinions, imaginations, and creativity into e-government operations. Also, this service provides people with the most convenient public services by enabling them to gain access to the services whenever and wherever they want.

In the case of the Seoul Metropolitan Government (SMG), under the vision and slogan of "Ubiquitous Seoul, World Class e-Government," SMG is trying to make the best use of ICTs and ubiquitous technology, and developing a variety of citizen-driven ICT services. Jung-hee Song, assistant Mayor for IT, is working on the front line to tackle these challenging tasks. Since 2006, the "Seoul Oasis" site is one of the successful services that have originated from the combination of citizens' imagination, creativity and digital technology (Anderson & Cho, 2010). Any citizen can freely make a suggestion on the site and if an idea attracts people's attention, the proposer, citizen customers, and experts get together to discuss and review the idea, and adopt it as a city policy if it is approved. In addition to making suggestions, citizens themselves are able to participate directly in the process of transforming their ideas into city policies.

Electronic government is not an opportunity to get a form via the Internet. It is the opportunity to get a government service without leaving your room, that's the point.
– Prime Minister, Dmitry Anatolyevich Medvedev, Russian Federation

D. Anderson et al., *E-Government Strategy, ICT and Innovation for Citizen Engagement*, SpringerBriefs in Electrical and Computer Engineering,
DOI 10.1007/978-1-4939-3350-1_4

In China, the government is also trying to enhance local government performances. Shanghai has one of China's leading local e-governments, with a wide range of e-government initiatives including website portal, e-procurement system, and a social security card system, etc. In this way, the Shanghai government has begun to provide e-government services, moving away from old static information services to dynamic interactive services with new technologies. The Shanghai government has developed a smart card system, in which citizens can access a variety of government-to-citizen (G2C) services with a social security card. The Shanghai government expects that the administration of social security and citizen services will serve as a new stimulus to the municipality's economy and strengthen China's transformation (Shi, 2007; Chen, Pan, Zhang, Huang, & Zhu, n.d.).

E-government can be transitional (gradual and evolutionary) or transformational (rapid and radical). Many developed countries like the United States falls in the transitional e-government mode. These are the early ICT adopters who have gone through a several iterations of ICTs in government and made a significant investment and dedicated resources over time. During the pre e-government days, these were the leaders who used technologies to manage government databases. Some of them learned the value of ICTs from each successive iteration of ICT transition.

In some cases, this learned knowledge is not useful as new disruptive technology completely changes the way things used to be. It can also keep a government that has invested too much in legacy systems from changing to a new, more efficient system early. In a cable interview with Eric Ken Shinseki, the Secretary of US Department of Veterans Affairs said that his department is still largely "driven by a paper-bound process." (CNN American Morning, November 11, 2009). He pointed out that the lack of system integration among departments and agencies was the main problem.

The transformational mode is based on a national strategy to achieve an effective e-government through rapid reform in legislation, dedication of resources, and smart use of ICTs. Both developed (without a long history of ICTs in the government) and less-developed (resource enriched) countries can be transformational if these conditions are met. Estonia, for example, which ranked 20th in the UN's 2012 e-Government Readiness Index,[1] falls into the transformational mode, making remarkable progress since its independence in 1991 (Table 4.1. UN 2010 e-Government Readiness Index).

4.2 Case Study

Following are six case studies, one for each region. The case studies were selected based on International Telecommunication Union's (ITU) "Measuring the Information Society 2011"[2] report. The selected countries ranked first in their respective regions: Korea, Sweden, US, UAE, Russia, and Mauritius.

---

[1] http://www.unpan.org/egovkb/global_reports/08report.htm

[2] https://www.itu.int/en/ITU-D/Statistics/Documents/publications/mis2013/MIS2013_without_Annex_4.pdf

Table 4.1 Top 10 EGDI rankings: 2012 and 2014

Country	Region	2014 e-government development index (EGDI)	2014 rank	2012 rank
Republic of Korea	Asia	0.9462	1	1
Australia	Oceania	0.9103	2	12
Singapore	Asia	0.9076	3	10
France	Europe	0.8938	4	6
Netherlands	Europe	0.8897	5	2
Japan	Asia	0.8874	6	18
United States of America	Americas	0.8748	7	5
United Kingdom	Europe	0.8695	8	3
New Zealand	Oceania	0.8644	9	13
Finland	Europe	0.8449	10	9

The case studies provide an overview of the infrastructure, type of government, level of transparency and e-government strategy. The examples of e-government initiatives focus on the following types of services: health, education, financial services and social services (Table 4.2).

4.2.1 Case Study: South Korea

After two decades of striving for informatization, Korea has earned a title as one of the most advanced countries in terms of ICT. Korea has actively pursued e-government as a crucial means to make the government more competitive by leveraging the world's best information technology (Fig. 4.1).

In 2003, the South Korean government, in considering e-government as a strategic tool for administrative reform and civil service innovation, chose 31 e-government roadmap projects as a part of the key national projects to be actively promoted from the very beginning of its term. As a result, most of the internal administrative affairs of the government can be processed electronically, and the efficiency, stability, and expertise of government resource management have been greatly improved.

Moreover, the government made connections to relevant systems (such as the Internet) for better information sharing or a non-stop or one-stop service environment. Also, it reduced document submissions for civil service applications and it increased the convenience and participation of its citizens in policy-making by providing portal services for civil applications. E-government is enabling citizens to interact with public offices without having to visit these offices in person.

South Korea's e-government promotion had focused on improving the efficiency in administrative affairs, but shifted its focus to improving citizens satisfaction

Table 4.2 Overview of six countries for case study

	Countries					
		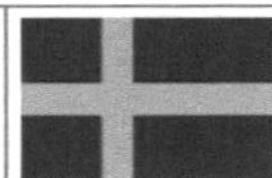				
Comparison criteria	Republic of Korea	Sweden	United States	UAE	Russia	Mauritius
Government type	Constitutional republic	Constitutional monarchy	Federal constitutional republic	Presidential federation of absolute hereditary monarchies	Presidential and parliamentary republic	Parliamentary representative democratic republic
ICT[a]	High (8.57)[b]	High (8.45)	High (7.53)	High (6.41)	High (6.19)	Upper (4.55)
E-Government Strategies	Yes	Yes	Yes	Yes	Yes	Yes
Transparency[c]	55	89	73	69	28	52
Online Service Index[d]	0.9764	0.7008	0.9449	0.8819	0.7087	0.4724
Telecommunication Infrastructure Index[d]	0.9350	0.8866	0.7406	0.5932	0.6413	0.4406
Human Capital Index[d]	0.9273	0.8802	0.9390	0.6657	0.8388	0.6882

[a]International Telecommunication Union (ITU) categorizes ICT development level of different countries by ICT Development Index score (1–10) in 2012 into high (6.19–8.57), upper (4.17–6.11), medium (2.40–4.11) and low (0.99–2.33)

[b]ICT Development Index score of 2012 by ITU

[c]The 2013 Corruption Perceptions Index (0–100) by Transparency International http://cpi.transparency.org/cpi2013/results/

[d]UN e-government survey 2014

Fig. 4.1 The Republic of Korea government portal

toward government services. It also improved economic feasibility, expertise and security of government resource management by constructing government-wide data centers and integrating government information systems. Since 2003, e-government has been extending people's active participation in the government affairs while driving IT industry development. E-government is now established and considered to be an indispensible component of government's management system that serves as an infrastructure for developing and improving the foundation for a democratic society and national competitiveness.

The aims of e-government have shifted from "promotion" and "construction" to improving "utilization" and "connection." In 2008, the Korean government finalized "The 4th National Informatization Master Plan",[3] which provides for five main goals including e-government development goals. The 'efficient knowledge government' envisioned by the Korean government provides services that can communicate with the citizens and support substantial value-creation for citizens and businesses. It also integrates and interconnects information systems of entire governmental departments and ministries in order to provide customer-oriented services while making operations more efficient.

In February 2011, the Korean government announced a new generation of e-government strategy, and government services will be delivered to the people at any time and place (Table 4.3).[4]

[3] http://unpan1.un.org/intradoc/groups/public/documents/un-dpadm/unpan045778~1.pdf

[4] http://english.seoul.go.kr/wp-content/uploads/2014/06/Seoul-e-Government-English.pdf

Table 4.3 History of Korea's e-government promotion, 2010 information white paper, National Information Society Agency, 2011

Phase	Period	Event	Achievement
First introduction	1978~1987	Computerization of administrative system	First and second phase administrative system computerization projects (1978~1986)
	1987~1996	Construction of national backbone network	First and second phase national backbone construction projects (1987~1996)
Foundation building	1996~2000	Informatization promotion	Foundation-building for high-speed information and communications (1995~2005) Constructed optical transmission network in 144 zones nation-wide Unit or function-based Informatization Procurement, passport, patent, customs, etc.
Project Initiation	2001~2002	Eleven initiatives for e-government	Eleven initiative tasks for electronic civil application, e-procurement, etc. Partial and limited connection between unit tasks
Growth	2003~2007	Thirty-one roadmap projects for e-government	Implemented 31 e-government roadmap projects under participation of multiple ministries (2003~2007) Amendment of e-Government Act (Jan. 2007)
Maturity	2008~present	Expansion of integration and connection	e-government promotion based on utilization and integration Expansion of target organizations to administrative institutions, public offices, and some private-sector organizations Unification of frameworks for national informatization and E-government implementation

4.2.1.1 Strategy

Korea has one of the most comprehensive, mature and high performance e-government programs in the world. For more than a decade, Korea has pursued a robust e-government program and with a great deal of consistency. Korea has constantly modified its strategy to accommodate emerging trends in both public sector operations and new technologies.

One of the strengths of the Korean strategy has been its vision and its completeness. The Korean strategy embraces all aspects of modern e-government programs – work method reform (transparency), government service reform (efficiency through automated government services; e.g., postal service, automated petition and policy

Table 4.4 Internet users, population and Facebook statistics for South Korea, internet live stats

Country	Population (July, 2014 Est.)	Internet users (July, 2014 Est.)	Internet penetration (% population)	Facebook (31-Dec-2012)	Facebook penetration (% population)
Republic of Korea	49,512,026	45,314,248	91.52 %	10,012,400	20.5 %

making) and information resource management reforms (participatory democracy).[5] The level of e-coordination on such a large scale for the country is unprecedented.

To a large extent, the mobilization to create functioning systems of e-government stems from Korea's culture. However, there has also been considerable innovation. For example, the early establishment of an "Informatization Promotion Committee" chaired by the Prime Minister[6] coupled with Korea's heightened sense of national identity has succeeded in inculcating a "u-ethos" across the entire nation.[7]

By achieving a common strategic purpose early on in the development of the e-government program in Korea, it has created stability among the various stakeholders to pursue a consistent, coherent and collaborative effort in creating a sustainable and dominant knowledge based economy within the next two decades.

4.2.1.2 Infrastructure

Recent increases in the use of wireless Internet technology and the rapid proliferation of smart phones have significantly changed the manner and mode of disseminating information (Table 4.4). In October 2011, Korea's smart phone users exceed 20 million (Fig. 4.2). The widespread usage of mobile devices has spawned new industries providing a variety of services and content, including in the areas of transportation, living, education, health, and gaming.

E-government services also need mobile services that can transcend the constraints of time and space. In February 2011, Ministry of Public Administration and Security announced 'Smart e-Government Promotion Plan' as a new generation of e-government strategy. Establishing Korea as a frontrunner in mobile e-governance was a top priority.[8] The government tries to provide personalized public services by increasing access to government policies and information, thus expanding channels for public participation and communication, and connecting or integrating services.

Additionally, the Korean government aims to preemptively respond to changes in the informatization paradigm by adopting new information technologies, and by

[5] http://english.seoul.go.kr/wp-content/uploads/2014/06/Seoul-e-Government-English.pdf

[6] http://unpan1.un.org/intradoc/groups/public/documents/un-dpadm/unpan042711.pdf

[7] http://www.e-service-expert.com/e-Government-Korea.html

[8] http://unpan1.un.org/intradoc/groups/public/documents/un-dpadm/unpan042711.pdf

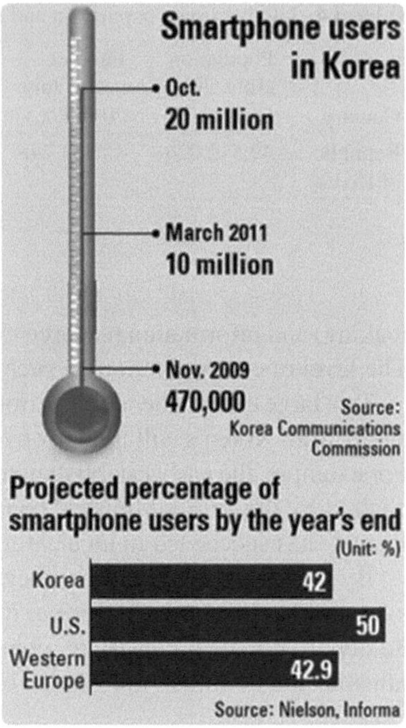

Fig. 4.2 Smartphone users in Korea

improving the level of government services to adapt to future changes in the social environment. It will be extended to build a sustainable e-government infrastructure so that government services are ubiquitous and responsive to the needs of the citizens.

4.2.1.3 Transparency

Another pervasive issue between government-citizen interactions is the status of citizen requests made to government. Many citizens wish to know the progress and procedures of the government service for which they have applied. In some cases, citizens have contacted civil servants directly to inquire of the progress of their applications. There can be an appearance of impropriety that arises from such practices, as it could be perceived as an illicit deal between a civilian and civil servant. As such, Korea's government has established administrative transparency as a top priority in the implementation of its e-government regime.[9]

The procedures and progress of a government administrative service is shown to citizens through the government service processing online public system for easier monitoring of their government applications. Currently, government bureaus as well as local governments have made information about the citizens' applications,

[9] http://unpan1.un.org/intradoc/groups/public/documents/UNGC/UNPAN043625.pdf

Fig. 4.3 Korea national portal, m.korea.go.kr

processing statuses, and the name of the supervising civil servant available on the Internet in real-time. In the long-run, the benefits are expected to be more than cost-savings, as efficiency, government-civilian interactions are all improved.

4.2.1.4 Practices

- **Mobile Government Cases**

The rapid spread of the use of mobile services has led the public sector to provide services, including the national portal (m.korea.go.kr), to inform the public about important aspects of their lives. Legal information, job information, municipal tourism, communications, transportation information, etc. are some of the areas covered by these mobile services (Fig. 4.3). The widespread use of mobile services is expected to have a significant impact on m-government and its subsequent development.

- **Seoul Metropolitan Government**

E-government has achieved significant improvements through the deployment of many innovative applications. Citizens use government web sites as central points of access to government information and services across different agencies via

Fig. 4.4 Seoul mobile portal m.Seoul

Internet access. The Seoul Metropolitan Government (SMG) has started the public online services for citizens since 2003.[10] However, the tech-savvy citizens of Seoul were not completely satisfied with the online services, which were generally available either at home or at work.

Koreans desired ubiquitous public services available from anywhere and at anytime. In particular, the people demanded fast access to information, such as traffic conditions and cultural events, even available to them while they were on-the-move. The necessary drivers for the mobile government include mobile device penetration, wireless Internet, and mobile net applications and services. With the high rate of penetration of mobile devices among Korean citizens, SMG launched ⓂSeoul702 (http://m.seoul.go.kr), a mobile portal built and run by the government to provide access to the highly demanded public services and contents, and to allow citizen participation (Fig. 4.4).

For instance, to report unlawful activities (e.g., dumping a bag of trash in an area not designated for waste), a citizen wishing to report the incident no longer needed to wait until they returned home so that they could access the Internet. Instead, the citizen's civic duty can be easily discharged by dialing "702" on their mobile device, followed by the Internet connection key, followed by an upload of a photo of the scene with the rubbish bag. Citizens can also leave a short text message about the nuisance using an appropriate menu link.

[10] http://english.seoul.go.kr/wp-content/uploads/2014/06/Seoul-e-Government-English.pdf

Table 4.5 Services used by menu

Traffic	14,919,705
Jobs	561,895
Culture/travel	333,205
Environment	150,037
Government information	171,766
Idea/suggestion	202,336
Tax	345,325
Others	497,905

A Korean citizen can access a total of 48 public services as of December 2010, ranging from participation in civic affairs, traffic information, cultural and weather information, e-Tax, public facility booking and city government news (Table 4.5).[11] All of this information is provided on a real-time basis.

In order to provide interactive communication, the government created different service menus through which the people can suggest ideas, make complaints, get experts' opinions and cast a vote for policies. Korean government officials have an efficient portal to gather the feedback of their constituents. With this feature, ⓂSeoul702 played a significant role in realizing participatory democracy in the municipal government by means of mobile phones, and ⓂSeoul702 is a client-centric service that reflects individual citizens' interests and lifestyles.

- **Comprehensive Tax Services** (www.hometax.go.kr)

Korea's Home Tax Service is a system for imposing, collecting, deducting, and exempting of internal taxes online, as well as inquiring of various tax related information. Through the Home Tax Service, taxpayers in the Republic of Korea can check their mobile phones to see what has been filed electronically by their agents on a real-time basis. Home Tax Service users subscribing to electronic billing service can also retrieve billing information. Information about unclaimed tax refunds for the past 5 years can also be retrieved. Citizens can also retrieve the business type and operation status of businesses by entering the business registration number (Fig. 4.5).

- **Internet Civil Services** (www.minwon.go.kr)

The Republic of Korea provides frequently used civil application services through smart phones. Citizens can now view the statuses of their applications regardless of time and place. Rather than visiting a public office, they can access the information from their mobile devices (OECD/International Telecommunication Union, 2011).

[11] http://unpan1.un.org/intradoc/groups/public/documents/un-dpadm/unpan047499.pdf

Fig. 4.5 Comprehensive tax services, www.hometax.go.kr

Particularly conducive to the use of m-government services are the mobile security features, which encrypt communications and personal information. These security features also prohibit storage of processed information.

It provides detailed information about 5,300 types of services. Also, up to 3,020 types of civil services are able to be requested by citizen at home without visiting administrative offices. The results of requested services are also informed by email and 1,208 types of civil documents are issued online, allowing citizens to print necessary official documents at home (OECD/International Telecommunication Union, 2011).

- **Electronic Procurement Service** (www.g2b.go.kr)

The Korean government started an electronic procurement service. It is a single window of procurement, called KONEPS (Korea Online e-Procurement System), which handles all procurement procedures online with the aim of improving efficiency and transparency of public procurement.[12]

In KONEPS, all stages of procurement, such as bidding, awarding contracts, contracting, delivery, and payment, are handled online, and procurement process can be monitored in real-time. Also, the registered companies are able to participate

[12] http://www.pps.go.kr/eng/jsp/koneps/overview.eng

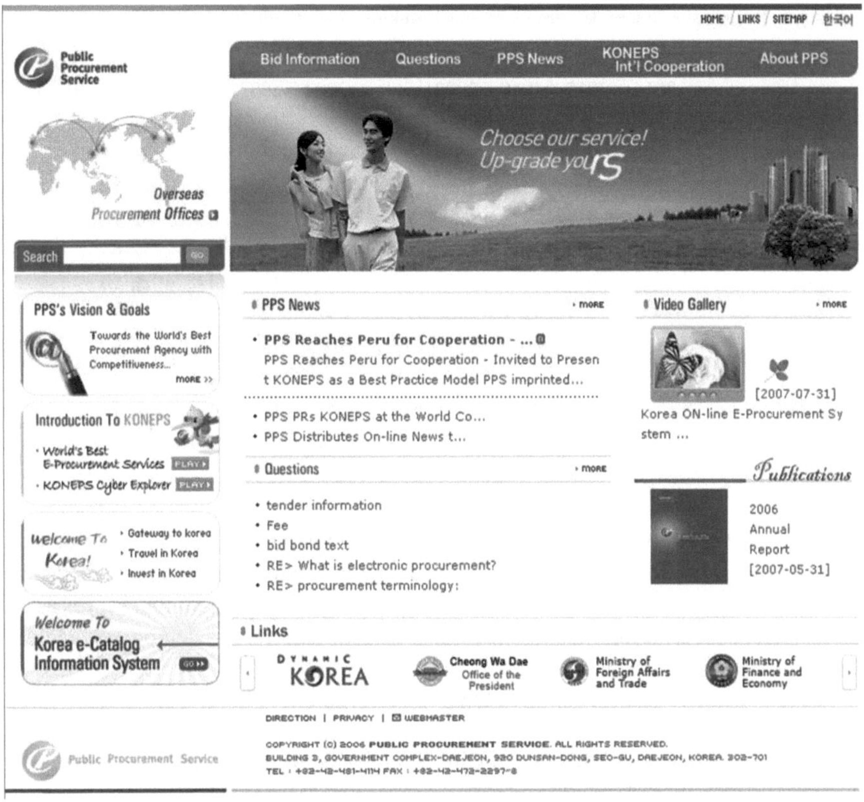

Fig. 4.6 Electronic procurement service, www.g2b.go.kr

in biddings of all public organizations, including central and local governments, and public organizations, by a single registration in the G2B system.

The KONEPS system has reached major milestones, including U.S. dollar value of transactions processed amounting to $75 billion annually, while 97 % of bidding is done electronically (Fig. 4.6). In the Future, all procedures from request for bidding to payment will be monitored in real time, and a RFID-based inventory management system will be established to provide safe and convenient electronic procurement service.

The e-government promotion led to enhanced efficiency of public administration by stabilizing electronic processing of government work. E-government has improved economic feasibility, expertise, and security of government resource management by constructing government-wide data centers and integrating government information systems. Moreover, it led to reductions in the volume of document submissions for civil service applications and it increased the convenience to citizens and the participation of citizens in policy-making by increasing citizen mobility.

The value of e-government implementation has changed from the vision of the 1990s in enhancing efficiency of public administration through computerization of

Table 4.6 UN e-government development index rankings top 10 countries (2012)

Country	Ranking by year								Rank difference (2001~2014)
	2014	2012	2010	2008	2005	2004	2003	2001	
Republic of Korea	1	1	1	6	5	5	13	15	▲ 14
Netherlands	5	2	5	5	12	11	11	8	▲ 3
UK	8	3	4	10	4	3	5	7	▽ 1
Denmark	16	4	7	2	2	2	4	9	▽ 7
US	7	5	2	4	1	1	1	1	▽ 6
France	4	6	10	9	23	24	19	14	▲ 10
Sweden	14	7	12	1	3	4	2	11	▽ 3
Norway	13	8	6	3	10	10	7	5	▽ 8
Finland	10	9	19	15	9	9	10	13	▲ 3
Singapore	3	10	11	23	7	8	12	4	▲ 1
Canada	11	11	3	7	8	7	6	6	▽ 5
Australia	2	12	8	8	6	6	3	2	–

government works to the millennium goals focused on increasing satisfaction and active participation of citizens into policy-making. Today, e-government is established and considered as the government's key management system that serves as an infrastructure for developing and improving the foundation for a democratic society and national competitiveness.

Korea's tireless efforts in advancing e-government and m-government have yielded dividends. Korea has been recognized as one of the global e-government leaders – obtaining the highest scores in "E-government Development Index" and "E-participation Index".[13] Korea's E-government Development Index ranking assessed by the United Nations improved from 15th in 2001 to the top in 2012 out of 190 countries worldwide, and its E-participation index ranking was also ranked 1st in 2012 (Table 4.6).

The results of Korea's e-government services are selected as the best practices and their excellence is being acknowledged by the rest of the world. For example, with the e-customs system called UNI-PASS that was established to complete an online export and import system for the first time in the world, Korea Customs Service won the WCO (World Customs Organization) Trophy in 2006 for intellectual property right protection with the fastest customs system among 169 member countries.

4.2.2 Case Study: Sweden

4.2.2.1 Government Type

Sweden is a constitutional monarchy with a representative democracy based on a parliamentary system of government. The Monarch has no political power. Legislative power is held by a unicameral parliament (Riksdagen). The Government

[13] http://unpan3.un.org/egovkb/en-us/Reports/UN-E-Government-Survey-2014

holds executive power, headed by the Prime Minister and responsible to the Riksdag. The Government determines its policies and sets its priorities.[14]

In total, there are three levels of Public Administration in Sweden: approximately 400 Central Government agencies, 21 Regional Government authorities (county councils) and 290 Local Government authorities (municipalities). Sweden became a member of the European Union on January 1, 1995.[15]

4.2.2.2 Strategies

The report released in December 2010 "Digitizing Public Services in Europe: Putting ambition into action – 9th Benchmark Measurement"[16] conducted for the European Commission, underlined that Sweden has five top strategic e-government priorities for the year ahead:

- Getting more and better integrated eServices in place.
- Implementing an updated system for eID.
- Financing of inter-agency projects.
- Continued service orientation of public agencies and organizations.
- Putting a new governance structure for e-government in place.

The e-government Delegation in Sweden later published two strategic reports: *As simple as possible for as many as possible: Under construction – future e-government* (SOU 2010:62) and *As simple as possible for as many as possible – Making progress* (SOU 2011: 27) [17] to further lead e-government strategy in the country. The overarching aims of the broader Swedish e-government program, as presented through these documents, are to:

- Make it as simple as possible for as many people as possible to exercise their rights, fulfill their obligations and access public administration services
- Strengthen the overall development capacity and innovative power of society
- Achieve flexible e-government that is based on users' needs.

The eDelegation's suggestions, in order to facilitate the realization of the Strategy's goals, covered the following aspects:

- eIdentification: the creation of a single and unified eID solution to access government services. This solution could be used within the framework of private sector services eventually. The Tax Board (Skatteverket), through a newly established committee, would coordinate the management of eIdentification,

[14] https://sweden.se/society/the-swedish-system-of-government/

[15] https://joinup.ec.europa.eu/sites/default/files/06/4b/a0/eGov%20in%20SE%20-%20May%202014%20-%2016.0.pdf

[16] http://ec.europa.eu/information_society/eeurope/i2010/docs/benchmarking/eGovernement_benchmarking_Method_paper_2010.pdf

[17] http://www.edelegationen.se/Documents/Remisser,%20bet%C3%A4nkanden%20mm/Summary_of_SOU_2010_20_0.pdf

and issue regulations on eID cards and the electronic data exchange between the public authorities.

- Launch of an Internet forum where citizens and businesses would be given the opportunity to take part in the shaping of future e-government.
- Several of the existing Public Agencies would be mandated to quickly and effectively develop specific e-government services. The public authorities should interact among them and with the private stakeholders in the aim to jointly develop common eServices.
- Better technical/legal rules and regulations to promote the use of eIdentification and eServices.
- The Public Agencies should select open standards first and always consider open source software.
- Some Public Agencies would be in charge of systematically monitoring the development and the testing of IT, so as to create the conditions for informed technological choices across the public administration.
- Clearer management and funding mechanisms for e-government projects. Specific funding should be earmarked for those strategic projects which could prove beneficial to third parties.
- Effective support service and shared service centers: the Tax Board and the National Police are currently participating in a pilot scheme aimed at developing the known as "administrative support activities" applied to financial and human resources.

4.2.2.3 Infrastructure

Sweden ranks No. 2 in the ICT development level after Republic of Korea in 155 countries around the world.[18] With 90 % of the population using the Internet (Table 4.7), Sweden is among the top five countries online, along with Iceland, Norway, the Netherlands and Luxembourg. Sweden is also among the world's top 10 in commercial fiber-to-the-home penetration. Such extensive fiber deployments have been achieved through a successful public-private strategy that has involved both private operators and local authorities. Mobile-broadband penetration is among the highest in the world (after the Republic of Korea and Japan).

Recent data show that there are now almost as many mobile-broadband subscriptions as fixed-broadband in Sweden, and that mobile data traffic continues to grow strongly, with an increase of just over 90 % in 2009. (Markendahl et al. 2009). This indicates that mobile-broadband uptake and usage is matching that of fixed broadband. Sweden also enjoys relatively low costs for these communication services (ranks 16th among 165 countries).

[18] http://www.itu.int/en/ITU-D/Statistics/Documents/publications/mis2012/MIS2012_without_Annex_4.pdf

Table 4.7 Internet users, population and Facebook statistics for Sweden, internet world stats

Country	Population (July, 2014 Est.)	Internet users (July, 2014 Est.)	Internet penetration (% population)	Facebook (31-Dec-2012)	Facebook penetration (% population)
Sweden	9,631,261	8,581,261	89.1 %	4,950,160	54.4 %

	Economy	Fixed-telephone subscriptions per 100 inhabitants 2011	Fixed-telephone subscriptions per 100 inhabitants 2012	Mobile-cellular subscriptions per 100 inhabitants 2011	Mobile-cellular subscriptions per 100 inhabitants 2012	International Internet bandwidth Bit/s per Internet user 2011	International Internet bandwidth Bit/s per Internet user 2012	Percentage of households with computer 2011	Percentage of households with computer 2012	Percentage of households with Internet access 2011	Percentage of households with Internet access 2012
136	Sweden	47.5	45.5	121.3	122.6	*236'638*	*279'755*	91.6	92.0	90.6	92.0

	Economy	Percentage of individuals using the Internet 2011	Percentage of individuals using the Internet 2012	Fixed (wired)-broadband subscriptions per 100 inhabitants 2011	Fixed (wired)-broadband subscriptions per 100 inhabitants 2012	Active mobile-broadband subscriptions per 100 inhabitants 2011	Active mobile-broadband subscriptions per 100 inhabitants 2012
136	Sweden	94.0	94.0	32.1	32.2	97.4	101.3

Rank	Economy	IPB 2012	IPB 2011	Fixed-telephone sub-basket as a % of GNI p.c. 2012	Fixed-telephone sub-basket as a % of GNI p.c. 2011	Mobile-cellular sub-basket as a % of GNI p.c. 2012	Mobile-cellular sub-basket as a % of GNI p.c. 2011	Fixed-broadband sub-basket as a % of GNI p.c. 2012	Fixed-broadband sub-basket as a % of GNI p.c. 2011	GNI p.c., USD, 2011 (or latest available year)
10	Sweden	0.6	0.6	0.6	0.6	0.5	0.5	0.8	0.8	53'230

Top 10 in Europe

		E-gov. development index		World e-gov. development index	
Rank	Country	2014	2012	2014	2012
1	France	0.8938	0.8635	4	6
2	Netherlands	0.8897	0.1925	5	2
3	United Kingdom	0.8695	0.8960	8	3
4	Finland	0.8449	0.8505	10	9
5	Spain	0.8410	0.7770	12	23
6	Norway	0.8357	0.8593	13	8
7	Sweden	0.8225	0.8599	14	7
8	Estonia	0.8180	0.7987	15	20
9	Denmark	0.8162	0.8889	16	4
10	Iceland	0.7970	0.7835	19	22
Regional average		0.6936	0.7188		
World average		0.4712	0.4882		

4.2.2.4 Transparency: Main Portals of E-Government in Sweden

- 'sweden.gov.se' portal (Fig. 4.7)

This portal serves as the English language website of the Swedish Government and the government offices. It is designed to provide documents and records, information about current government bills, initiatives and ministerial activities, and accounts of how the decision-making process works in Sweden.

The website has three main sections:

- The Government and the Government Offices: The section offers up-to-date information listed according to each ministry, minister and subject area.
- Publications: This section contains all information material and other publications issued in English or other foreign languages (along with an ordering facility).

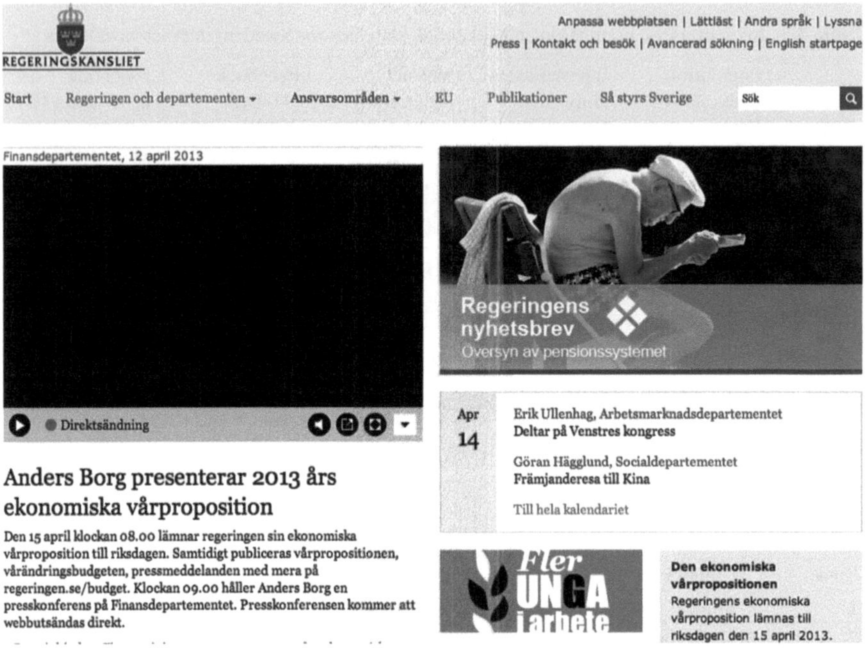

Fig. 4.7 Sweden government portal

- How Sweden is governed: This section places the work of the Government and the Government Offices in context. Decision-making processes, the EU and other matters are described and exemplified.
- "verksamt.se" portal: the Swedish Business Link to Government

The "verksamt.se" portal (Fig. 4.8) provides a comprehensive single-point for entrepreneurs and enterprises to access relevant and official eServices and information from three public authorities: the Swedish Companies Registration Office (Bolagsverket); the Swedish Tax Agency (Skatteverket); and the Swedish Agency for Economic and Regional Growth (Tillväxtverket).

This initiative develops, improves, joins and replaces two existing eServices; the online guidance for those willing to start or run a business (Företagarguiden) and the company registration service (Foretagsregistrering). "Verksamt.se" joins up the guidance and information parts with both the company registration and company tax filing eServices. Furthermore, it introduces a new tool to create a business plan, where information can be transferred and re-used in other eServices.

- 'sweden.se' portal

This is the official gateway to Sweden (Fig. 4.9). Through this portal all interested parties can gather information on working and starting a business in Sweden. The service also provides the ability to download forms and applications.

In 2009, a section on the website of the Swedish Government provided general information on measures taken in different sectors, such as warranty programs for

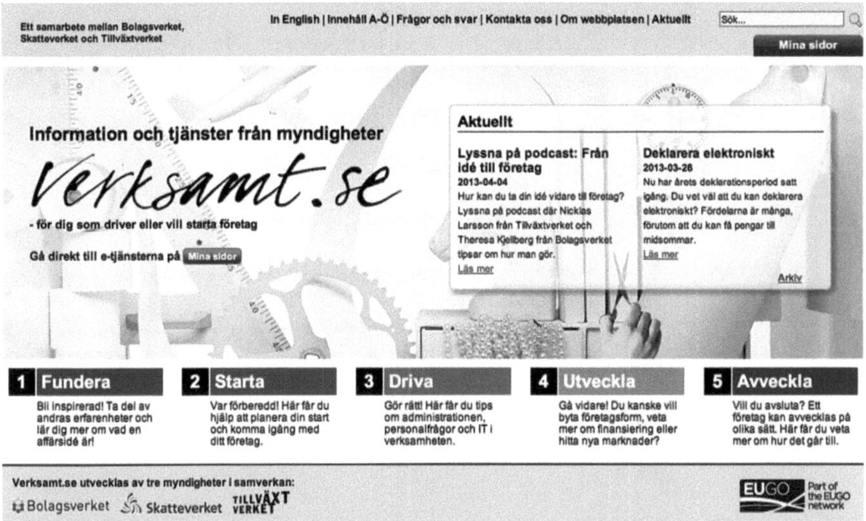

Fig. 4.8 The Swedish business link to government

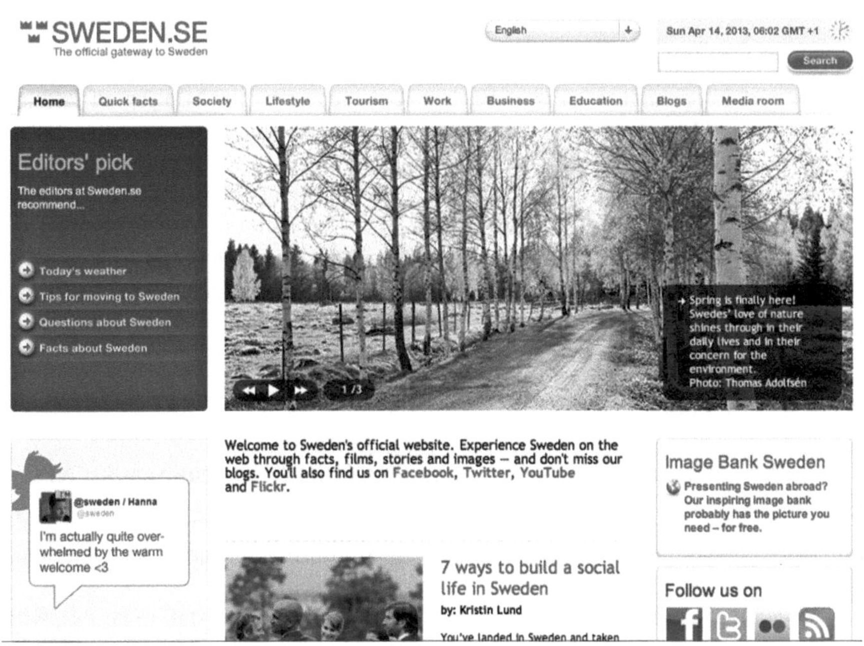

Fig. 4.9 'sweden.se' portal

financial institutions and support for Swedish municipalities. Citizens can recognize transparency – and the lack thereof – when they see it, and providing the public with more and better information on decisions taken and the reasons for them is a major need to be addressed by governments.

Fig. 4.10 ‘openaid.se’ portal

- “openaid.se” portal

The portal “openaid.se” (Fig. 4.10) has been created by the Ministry of Foreign Affairs to provide information on the aid Sweden gives to other countries. The portal enables organizations, journalists and the public to trace the entire process of giving aid from the preparation of aid efforts through decisions and reports to the evaluation of the tasks undertaken. The immediate goal is to increase transparency on aid as a way of boosting the fight against poverty. Information from as far back as 1975 is available, although the information becomes more detailed and complete for the more recent years.

4.2.2.5 Practices

- **The National Patient Summary program (Nationell Patientöversikt: NPÖ)**

The context behind the NPÖ (Fig. 4.11) is the need for efficient tools that enable authorized health professionals to access patient information across organizational boundaries.

The National Patient Summary enables qualified healthcare staff to access, with the patient’s consent, online medical records filed by other caregivers and thereby obtain a comprehensive snapshot of the patient’s health. This provides a better basis for diagnosis, treatment and monitoring while facilitating healthcare coordination between the healthcare professionals involved. NPÖ is the first of such common, countrywide healthy solutions and a “plough” for the development of the required security solutions and infrastructure.

Fig. 4.11 Nationell patientöversikt – NPÖ

The NPÖ project is intended to improve four key aspects of healthcare:

- Quality: Having an overall picture of a patient's previous diagnoses, test results and medication facilitate accurate diagnosis and the timely prescription of proper treatment. It also provides better opportunities to take preventative measures and to coordinate healthcare efforts across the county or the municipality, and with private healthcare providers.
- Safety: The right decision support reduces the risk of medical (e.g. medication) errors. Awareness of a patient's adverse reactions to agents or substances makes it possible to avoid risks and patient discomfort. The patient's assessment and treatment are both facilitated, even in emergency situations where there is no time to wait for information from other healthcare providers.
- Efficiency: Shared information reduces the costs related to taking samples or performing tests several times. Patients do not need to repeat their entire treatment history at a meeting with new healthcare providers, and medical records do not need to be sent by post.
- Increased patient involvement: patients gain increased influence as they can decide to block access to their information for given cares, and it is expected over time that patients will get a better insight into their own care.

The healthcare staff of the municipality of Örebro (southern Sweden) rates highly the National Patient Summary (Nationell patientöversikt – NPÖ, in Swedish) service (National Patient Summary, 2012). Nine out of ten NPÖ users are "satisfied" or "very satisfied" with it, and more than 60 % of them believe that it has been highly or very highly beneficial for their work, according to a recent survey conducted at the end of 2011.[19]

[19] National Patient Summary (http://www.epractice.eu/en/news/5347051).

However, there's still space of improvement for this appraised program: some users suggested that the IT service could be more user-friendly while others called for the access to information from several clinics and/or to most test results.

- **eInvoice Program**

On March 1, 2011, the "Pan-European Public Procurement Online" project (PEPPOL) reached an important milestone when the first invoice was successfully transferred via PEPPOL solutions. The central administrative agency Swedish National Financial Management Authority (ESV) received the invoice, which was issued by a Danish subcontractor. The transaction was done using the PEPPOL transport infrastructure for message transfer, and the PEPPOL Business Interoperability Specifications (BIS) for process descriptions and document content.

The central administrative agency Swedish National Financial Management Authority (ESV) received the invoice, which was issued by a Danish subcontractor. The transaction was done using the PEPPOL transport infrastructure for message transfer and the PEPPOL Business Interoperability Specifications (BIS) for process descriptions and document content. The invoice was successfully transferred and imported by ESV into the eInvoice workflow module of their Enterprise Resource Planning (ERP) system, where it was approved and paid. ESV is already currently working with domestic eInvoices and the scanning of paper invoices.

Compared to the scanning procedure, such electronic invoice saves times for manual work and increases efficiency. It also streamlines cross-border eInvoices with the processing and archiving of domestic electronic invoices.

Furthermore, use of the PEPPOL transport infrastructure and PEPPOL BIS makes it easier to conduct business electronically across borders, and have the potential to radically change the way eProcurement processes – not only eInvoicing – are being conducted between public sector buyers and their suppliers. It is also a significant step for the building of PEPPOL business community. ESV is now looking forward to connect more suppliers as this first transaction can be considered to be a milestone that proves the feasibility and usefulness of PEPPOL.[20]

- **The Development of Electronic Identification**

Currently there are three types of electronic identification (eID) cards used by Swedish citizens to access certain e-government services. Any physical person with a Swedish personal identity number can obtain an eID. This number appears on the eID and its microchip.

One is the personal and non-official electronic ID cards issued by the Swedish Post and software-based electronic IDs including the Bank ID.

The second one is the eID for legal entities. There are two types of certificates for such eID, namely the server and stamping certificates, for authentication and signing respectively. The certificates contain the name of the organization and the organizational number and may also contain a URL. The contact person ordering

[20] https://digitaliser.dk/pages/GroupView.aspx?panel=forum&commentPID=984761

organizational certificates must have an authorization for this purpose from a person authorized to sign on behalf of his/her organization.

Another type is called Steria eID: the organizational certificates for personal use. This type of certificate contains the organizational number, the name of the organization, as well as the name and the role of the person. It is worth noting that none of the organizational eIDs contain the personal ID number which is considered to be sensitive information.

Citizens now can even use their mobile phones to access public services via digital signatures and unique IDs. A mobile channel to find temporary daycare workers has been set up. This enables the integration of social welfare services, as citizens can access a range of services from their mobile phones via the Swedish online social welfare portal using eIDs and digital signatures.

On 18 August 2011 a test bed was launched to provide a means to publicly test and develop the technological infrastructure for eID and signing services in Sweden. The test bed, eID 2.0, was developed by the eIdentification Board (E-legitimationsnamnden) in collaboration with the Swedish University Computer Network (SUNET). It will enable interested parties (both public and private sector entities) to test their eServices and technology solutions for eID. Only after successful testing takes place, will it be possible to implement a functional infrastructure for eID.

However, one big issue confronting the usage of eID is that As the eIDs are issued by different suppliers, the authority which provides eServices must be able to authenticate users, verify eSignatures and apply for revocation checks in different ways and towards different eID-suppliers.

During June 2008, the Swedish Administrative Development Agency (Verva) published a series of proposals regarding eID Management in the long-term. The Agency proposed that the Government guarantee that there is a regulated system for eIDs which provides support for both qualified and advanced electronic signatures, provided that the terms “Swedish eID” and “Swedish official eID” are defined in a suitable manner in order to be given an adequate legal basis, and that a certification system is formulated for the proposed eIDs.

Last summer, Sweden’s eIdentification Board has set itself a goal of providing a mature eID solution by mid-2013. The Board currently is constructing a test environment to clarify stakeholders’ needs.

- **M-Government**

In November 2011, the Swedish employment agency Arbetsförmedlingen launched a free-of-charge application enabling smartphone holders to look for a job via their phones. The job ads app is the mobile version of the same agency’s online employment database Platsbanken, already proving popular (Fig. 4.12). It makes it possible for smartphone holders to:

- Search for a job by keyword, work location and profession;
- Save their searches and ads;
- Email and share job ads;
- Find the employer’s address on a map;
- Find all employment agencies in Sweden and their geographical location on a map.

Fig. 4.12 Platsbanken, Arbetsförmedlingen

Non-Swedish speakers will find the app useful as the text of the ads – apart from the work locations and the job titles – can be translated into Arabic, English, French, Russian and Spanish.

- **Education – Library 2007**

Through Library 2007, which is a new web site shared by libraries in six small municipalities in the Umeå region of Sweden, all citizens have been given the opportunity to reserve and borrow books, as well as to download e-books, music and films from the Web, 24/7 (Fig. 4.13).

With a pointing device and a wireless headset, the visitor can point at the book spine and hear the same information about the title, author and contents that is written on the book cover. Thus the visually impaired can search for books on the shelves themselves at the Umeå Public Library since the books "talk to the visitor" when they point at the book spine.

Today, the inhabitants of the Umeå region can borrow from a total stock of one million books and return items at any of the libraries in the region thanks to a single library card.[21] Thus, cooperation in the Umeå region has given the participating municipalities a considerable increase in book stock without having to purchase a single book. Borrowers can manage a great deal without even leaving their home, which has made the library a user-friendly environment. Accessibility has increased for borrowers in general, and the disabled in particular, thanks to the Talking Library application.

[21] http://unpan3.un.org/unpsa/Public_NominationProfile.aspx?id=399

Fig. 4.13 Library 2007

4.2.3 Case Study: United States

4.2.3.1 Government Type

The United States of America (commonly abbreviated to the United States, the U.S., USA, America, and the States) is a federal constitutional republic comprising 50 states and a federal district. The government is regulated by a system of checks and balances defined by the U.S. Constitution, which serves as the country's supreme legal document.[22] In the American federalist system, citizens are usually subject to three levels of government, federal, state, and local. The local government's duties are commonly split between county and municipal governments. In almost all cases, executive and legislative officials are elected by a plurality vote of citizens by district. There is no proportional representation at the federal level, and it is very rare at lower levels.

The federal government is composed of three branches[23]:

- Legislative: The bicameral Congress, made up of the Senate and the House of Representatives, makes federal law, declares war, approves treaties, has the power of the purse, and has the power of impeachment, by which it can remove sitting members of the government.

[22] U.S. Constitution, Article VI, Clause 2 ("Supremacy Clause").

[23] https://www.cia.gov/library/publications/the-world-factbook/geos/us.html

- Executive: The president is the commander-in-chief of the military, and the president can veto legislative bills before they become law. The president appoints the members of the cabinet (subject to U.S. Senate approval) and other officers who administer and enforce federal laws and policies.
- Judicial: The Supreme Court and lower federal courts, whose judges are appointed by the president with Senate approval, interpret laws and overturn those they find unconstitutional.

4.2.3.2 Infrastructure

The United States kept the same position (17th) over the 2-year period. The relatively low mobile-cellular and household Internet access penetration rates compared with most European countries have been one of the reasons. On the other hand, mobile broadband is increasingly rapidly in the country, and penetration rates rose to 54 % at the end of 2010, compared with 26 % at the end of 2008. Fixed-telephone services have been subsidized to ensure that all customers including rural and low-income customers have basic telephone access.

A discussion was launched recently in the United States on the possibility of moving from subsidized fixed telephony to subsidized broadband services. The United States recently redefined broadband as a "transmission service that actually enables an end user to download content from the Internet at 4 Mbps and to upload such content at 1 Mbps over the broadband provider's network." This is different from the definition by ITU and OECD that broadband as a connection with downstream speeds greater than, or equal to, 256 kbit/s.

As part of the new Cloud First Initiative, government agencies are required to consider cloud options before making new IT investments (Table 4.8).

4.2.3.3 Strategies

E-Government Act of 2002[24] Defines "electronic Government" (E-Government) as the use by Government of web-based Internet applications and other information technologies, combined with processes that implement these technologies, to: (1) enhance the access to and delivery of Government information and services; or (2) bring about improvements in Government operations. The Act offers a legal and political framework for future development of e-government in the United States:

To provide effective leadership of Federal Government efforts to develop and promote electronic Government services and processes by establishing an Administrator of a new Office of Electronic Government within the Office of Management and Budget.

---

[24] Amending 44 U.S.C. §§ 101 & 3501 et seq.; Creating 44 U.S.C. § 3541 et seq.; 44 U.S.C. § 3601 et seq.

Table 4.8 Internet users, population and Facebook statistics for the United States, internet world stats

Country	Population (July, 2014 Est.)	Internet users (July, 2014 Est.)	Internet penetration (% population)	Facebook (30-Sept-2012)	Facebook penetration (% population)
United States	322,583,006	279,834,232	86.75 %	166,029,240	52.9 %

	Economy	Fixed-telephone subscriptions per 100 inhabitants		Mobile-cellular subscriptions per 100 inhabitants		International Internet bandwidth Bit/s per Internet user		Percentage of households with computer		Percentage of households with Internet access	
		2011	2012	2011	2012	2011	2012	2011	2012	2011	2012
150	United States	45.8	44.0	95.3	98.2	47'174	62'274	77.2	79.3	71.7	75.0

	Economy	Percentage of individuals using the Internet		Fixed (wired)-broadband subscriptions per 100 inhabitants		Active mobile-broadband subscriptions per 100 inhabitants	
		2011	2012	2011	2012	2011	2012
150	United States	77.9	81.0	27.4	28.0	69.8	75.3

Rank	Economy	IPB		Fixed-telephone sub-basket as a % of GNI p.c.		Mobile-cellular sub-basket as a % of GNI p.c.		Fixed-broadband sub-basket as a % of GNI p.c.		GNI p.c., USD, 2011 (or latest available year)
		2012	2011	2012	2011	2012	2011	2012	2011	
8	United States	0.5	0.6	0.4	0.3	0.9	0.9	0.4	0.5	48'450

Top 10 in the Americas

Rank	Country	E-gov. development index 2014	E-gov. development index 2012	World e-gov. development index 2014	World e-gov. development index 2012
1	United States	0.8748	0.8687	7	5
2	Canada	0.8418	0.8430	11	11
3	Uruguay	0.7420	0.6315	26	50
4	Chile	0.7122	0.6769	33	39
5	Argentina	0.6306	0.6228	46	56
6	Colombia	0.6173	0.6572	50	43
7	Costa Rica	0.6061	0.5379	54	77
8	Brazil	0.6008	0.6167	57	59
9	Barbados	0.5933	0.6566	59	44
10	Antigua and Barbuda	0.5927	0.6345	60	49
Regional average		0.5074	0.5403		
World average		0.4712	0.4882		

- Promote use of the Internet and other information technologies to provide increased opportunities for citizen participation in Government.
- Promote inter-agency collaboration in providing electronic Government services, where this collaboration would improve the service to citizens by integrating related functions, and in the use of internal electronic Government processes, where this collaboration would improve the efficiency and effectiveness of the processes.
- Improve the ability of the Government to achieve agency missions and program performance goals.
- Promote the use of the Internet and emerging technologies within and across Government agencies to provide citizen-centric Government information and services.

- Reduce costs and burdens for businesses and other Government entities.
- Promote better informed decision-making by policy makers.
- Promote access to high quality Government information and services across multiple channels.
- Make the Federal Government more transparent and accountable.
- Transform agency operations by utilizing, where appropriate, best practices from public and private sector organizations.
- Provide enhanced access to Government information and services in a manner consistent with laws regarding protection of personal privacy, national security, records retention, access for persons with disabilities, and other relevant laws.

In the federal government's E-Government Strategy released in 2002,[25] the vision for reforming government emphasizes that "government needs to reform its operations – how it goes about its business and how it treats the people it serves." The vision is guided by three principles:

- Citizen-centered, not bureaucracy-centered;
- Results-oriented; and
- Market-based, actively promoting innovation.

In December 2010, the U.S. Chief Information Officer (CIO) published the 25 Point Implementation Plan To Reform Federal Information Technology Management,[26] based on collaboration with the Federal IT communities, industry experts and academics. The Plan outlines concrete steps that the Federal Government will take over the next 18 months to address the most pressing, persistent challenges plaguing Federal IT – ultimately delivering more value to the American taxpayer:

- Achieve operational efficiency – apply "Light Technology" and shared solutions
- Effectively manage large-scale IT program – strengthen program management, align the acquisition process and budget process with the technology cycle, streamline governance and improve accountability, and increase engagement with industry.

4.2.3.4 Transparency

The United States has come a long way since President Obama signed the Memorandum on "Transparency and Open Government"[27] on his first full day in office. One highlight of the Open Government Initiative has been the release of agency Open Government Plans. These plans have served as roadmaps for agencies working to expand opportunities for citizen participation, make data more available

---

[25] Information Technology and E-Government (2002) E-Government Strategy. USA GOV. http://www.usa.gov/Topics/Includes/Reference/egov_strategy.pdf

[26] Kundra V (2010) 25 Point Implementation Plan To Reform Federal Information Technology Management. CIO. http://cio.gov/documents/25-Point-Implementation-Plan-to-Reform-Federal%20IT.pdf

[27] https://www.whitehouse.gov/the_press_office/TransparencyandOpenGovernment

and transparent, and increase collaborative decision-making. Open government promotes a range of important goals[28]:

- The first goal is to increase accountability. As government becomes more open, both private and public institutions are more likely to be held accountable.
- The second goal is to provide people with information that they can readily find and use in their daily lives. Important information is being disclosed to the public in areas that involve product recalls, infant car seats, automobile safety, health care, energy, nutrition, air pollution, obesity, crime, and much more.
- The third goal is to use the dispersed knowledge of the American people. As the President has said, "Knowledge is widely dispersed in society, and public officials benefit from having access to that dispersed knowledge."

The United States is definitely one of the pioneering countries around the world in the construction of transparency, participation and collaboration for governmental administration. Here are some evidences and examples:

- USAspending.gov: USAspending is the only Government on-line source that makes Federal spending in contracts and grants visible to Congress, agencies, the public and better Government interest groups. It allows for information to be researched by firm, state, locality, congressional district, type of spending, and other categories.
- The IT Dashboard shows the Government, the public, and other stakeholders how Federal information technology investments are being made. By offering insight into the effectiveness of government technology programs, the IT Dashboard guides budget and policy decisions governing Federal IT.
- The creation of the data.gov website by the United States Government is one of the most substantial steps taken so far to provide a platform of open data for third parties. Launched in 2009, the website functions as a clearinghouse for datasets generated by the government in an accessible developer- friendly format. Similar feedback was sought for the second version of United States Recovery Act website by the United States Recovery Accountability and Transparency Board, which asked the community of developers for their views on the most convenient format for disclosing data on crisis-response funds.
- The Free File website allows most taxpayers to prepare and file their taxes online for free and get their refunds in half the time it would take to process their paper returns.

4.2.3.5 Practices

- **USA.gov**

The United States was found, as before, a best practice example of an integrated portal that provides a relatively easy navigation design and collects and consolidates

[28] Sunstein CR, Vein C (2012) Celebrating the Release of Open Government Plans 2.0. Whitehouse. http://www.whitehouse.gov/blog/2012/04/09/celebrating-release-open-government-plans-20

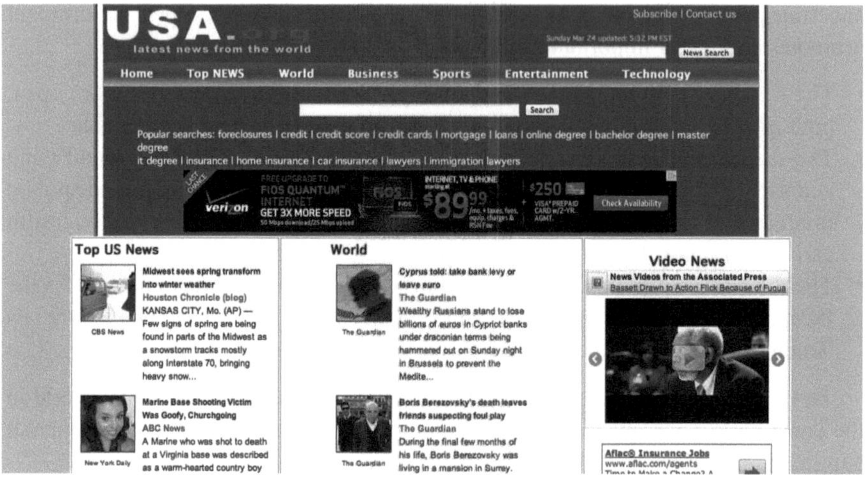

Fig. 4.14 US government portal

all information and services for citizens in one place, including agency services at the state and local levels. This vastly increases the effectiveness of user search and uptake. The national portal of the United States is a leader in e-government (Fig. 4.14).

The USA.gov homepage links to more than 100 online government services and transactions. A navigational tool bar organizes information in categories for citizens, business and non-profit organizations, government employees, and visitors to the country. It then breaks these categories down even further so users can quickly locate the information and services.

In addition, the national portal also offers its general information in 88 languages with extensive online services for foreigners wishing to conduct business, work, study and travel in the United States. It also includes live personal assistance via "Live Help/Web Chat". The site also makes it very easy to connect and communicate with the government via social media tools such as YouTube, Twitter, Facebook and the 'Gov Gab Blog', where bloggers share tips and information from the Federal government and where citizens can comment and share their own experiences.

- **Fostering social inclusion and increasing e-service usage through social media**

In the United States, social media usage has reached a milestone in 2011; two-thirds of adult Internet users (65 %) were using a social networking site, which means that half of all adults (50 %) use these.[29] According to the latest United States study, "embrace" of social media by the United States government seems to have "particular appeal" to minority groups, low-income individuals, women and other groups that have historically lagged behind in their use of e-services.[30] These groups all use

[29] http://www.pewinternet.org/files/old-media//Files/Reports/2011/PIP-SNS-Update-2011.pdf

[30] http://www.slideshare.net/undesa/united-nations-egovernment-survey-2012

Fig. 4.15 Smarter cabs

social media at a rate similar to that of other citizens, leading to a smaller gap among different socio-economic groups than through other forms of online information and service delivery. The government also launched a selection of applications that allow smartphone users to access its services while on-the-move.

The latest study found that 66 % of all United States Government agencies currently use some form of social networking. For example, more than 60 million followers subscribe to the Twitter feed of President Barack Obama. Politicians have been inclined to embrace and encourage the use of these e-participation and e-tools. They are providing information directly to citizens, which may help citizens to have a better understanding of their politicians.

- **Smarter Cabs in New York City**

In New York City, the Taxi & Limousine Commission (TLC) is now accepting proposals from software developers for a new app that lets passengers pay fares using their smartphone. The TLC envisions payment receipts being transmitted via email on this new system (Fig. 4.15).

Backseat TVs in 30 taxis will be replaced with iPads encased in metal sleeves, reports *The New York Times.*[31] The iPads will be attached to credit card swipers that passengers can use to pay for their ride at any point in their trip – even before the fare is calculated. Receipts will be sent to passengers' phones by email or text message. In addition to the payment capability, respondents are also encouraged to consider a points system with rewards for frequent riders, ridesharing possibilities and other enhanced customer service features.

Similar smartphone functionality is already in use or is being planned for other U.S. cities. In Alexandria, VA, passengers can book a cab and pay their fare using

---

[31] Bilton, Nick. (2012, March 6). With New Hardware, Square Begins Rollout. Retrieved: http://bits.blogs.nytimes.com/2012/03/06/with-new-hardware-square-begins-taxi-rollout/?_r=0

an app called Taxi Magic. According to Yellow Cab Cooperative, cab fare payment via smartphone is planned in San Francisco as well.[32]

- **Electronic Benefits Transfer (EBT)**

During Hurricane Katrina in New Orleans, some remarkably successful relief efforts were identified. Using its existing electronic benefits transfer (EBT) infrastructure, the Food and Nutrition Service in the U.S. Department of Agriculture worked with state governments and private EBT vendors to deliver $907 million in emergency food stamp benefits to 2.3 million households.[33] The American Red Cross provided emergency financial assistance to over 4 million survivors, amounting to some $1.5 billion in cash, checks, and electronic benefits by April 2006.

The EBT Council began in September 1995 as an organization composed of federal agencies, states, merchants, payments networks, financial institutions, and other EBT service providers, including consultants and processor (Fig. 4.16). The federal government, through the Office of Management and Budget, encouraged these stakeholders to meet in a deliberative group to develop operating rules for the electronic delivery of government benefits, including food stamp and cash benefits.

Currently all states and the District of Columbia offer statewide EBT programs, and 40 of these use the rules developed by the EBT Council, which is now known as the Electronic Benefits and Services (EBS) Council. Electronic Benefits Transfer was a critical means of delivering assistance to hundreds of thousands of people in the aftermath of Katrina. EBT has been implemented in all States since June of 2004.

- **iHealthRecord: An Online Medical Record Program**

iHealthRecord, an online health information resource launched in 2005, has great potential in terms of efficiency in case of emergency or simply when changing general practitioners. The new system allows patients to see, change and share medical records on the Internet through a service launched by a company set up by a coalition of professional medical groups (Fig. 4.17).

The service is a secure, confidential and interactive personal health record that stores personal health information for patients and also provides interactive programs that help people to better understand medical conditions and medications at no cost to patients. iHealthRecord permits patients to control their own records while allowing doctors vital access when they need it, eventually reducing the risks of mistakes, such as errors in prescriptions. It is hoped that the service can provide a way to replace thick medical charts and swap information without the need for costly, time-consuming office visits.

iHealthRecord could be a crucial first step to transforming the ponderous, mistake-prone and largely paper-based medical records system in the U.S. into an efficient, digital structure, which reduces medical errors and saves lives regardless

[32] Cabanatuan, Michael. (2014, September 23). S.F. Taxi Owners, Cabbies Join Forces Against Uber, Lyft, others. Retrieved: http://www.sfgate.com/bayarea/article/S-F-taxi-owners-cabbies-join-forces-against-5773407.php

[33] http://www.businessofgovernment.org/sites/default/files/StantonKatrinaReport.pdf

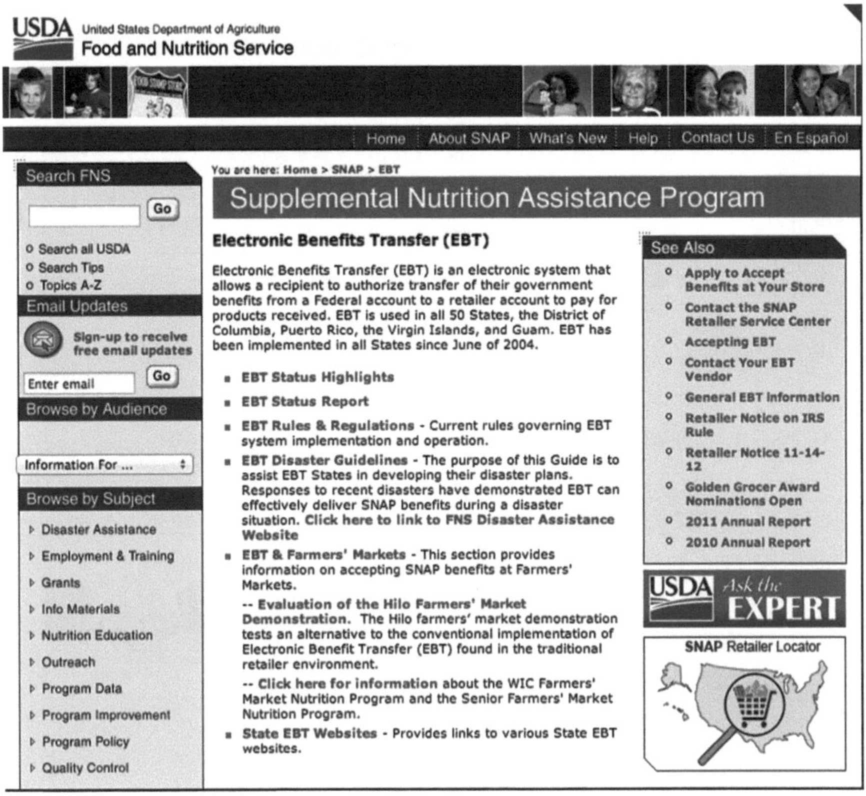

Fig. 4.16 Electronic benefits transfer (EBT)

of whether patients move or change health plans or doctors. The system is designed to minimize the risk that hackers could view patient records. However, there is a very small probability that patients could falsify online records if they wished or create phony profiles even if the real risk is very low.

- **Educator Licensure and Recruitment (ELAR) System**

The Educator Licensure and Recruitment (ELAR) project was defined to expand and improve the pool of teachers in the Commonwealth by removing bureaucratic and technological roadblocks for prospective educators. It is a critical component to help reshape license regulations and streamlining the application through an educator licensing process. The first version of ELAR enables the online application and approval of academic educator licenses. The second version of ELAR facilitates the educator recruitment process between the schools and educators/prospective educators. The third version includes licensing of vocational educators (Fig. 4.18).

The ELAR system addresses the vital need for a qualified educator in every classroom in every public school. It encourages individuals to pursue teaching and administrative careers. It creates an on-line process to inquire, apply for and receive

Fig. 4.17 iHealthRecord program

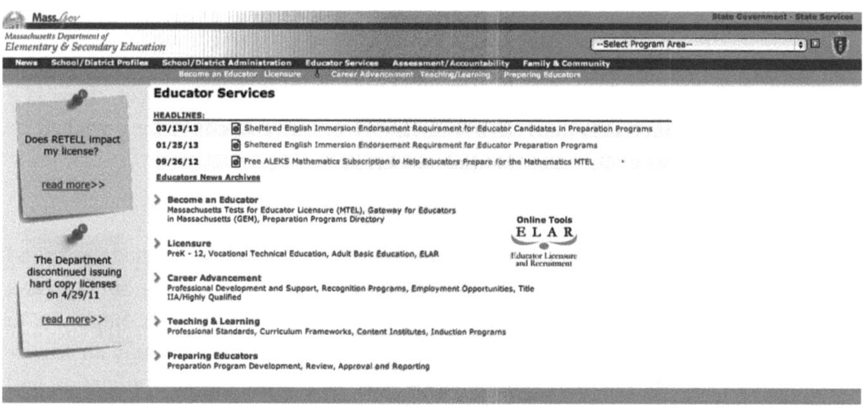

Fig. 4.18 Educator Licensure and Recruitment (ELAR) system

educator licenses, and it also creates a streamlined process for the state to process these requests, providing valuable services to superintendents and administrators who are searching for educators.

- **Sustainability**

The initiative Apps for Democracy, implemented in the United States by the District of Columbia, offers a pertinent example of the creation of sustainability through partnership between the public and government. Launched in 2008, Apps for Democracy featured a contest with awards for the best applications built upon data supplied by the district government. In 30 days, at a cost of $50,000 in awards, participants developed 47 applications that would have cost $2.6 million if developed internally by the District.[34] Such a model provides for high investment value while mobilizing and leveraging technological capabilities for public use, which are all factors that are important to the sustainability of the open data model.

E-government can also support environmental institutional integration by bringing environment agencies online and linking them with governance structures responsible for development planning so that coordinated solutions can be found while ensuring that those solutions ar efficient, effective and sustainable. One case is the e-catalog for procurement by government agencies in the United States, which has improved the tracking and monitoring of green purchases. The U.S. General Services Administration has been using social media tools to ask citizens how to improve the procurement of environmentally-friendly goods and services.

4.2.4 Case Study: United Arab Emirates

4.2.4.1 Government Type

The politics of the United Arab Emirates (UAE) take place in a framework of a federal, presidential system of a federation of absolute hereditary monarchies. The UAE is a federation of seven absolute monarchies: the emirates of Abu Dhabi, Ajman, Fujairah, Sharjah, Dubai, Ras al-Khaimah and Umm al-Qaiwain. The President of the United Arab Emirates is its head of state, and the Prime Minister of the United Arab Emirates is its head of government, including foreign affairs, security and defense, nationality and immigration issues, education, public health, currency, postal, telephone and other communications services, air traffic control, licensing of aircraft, labor relations, banking, delimitation of territorial waters and extradition of criminals. All responsibilities not granted to the national government are reserved to the emirates. The UAE government comprises three branches: the executive, legislature, and judiciary.[35]

[34] H.B. 5309. Testimony of William L. Vallée Jr., CT Broadband Policy & Programs Coordinator (March 12, 2012).

[35] http://self.gutenberg.org/articles/politics_of_the_united_arab_emirates

4.2.4.2 Infrastructure

The UAE ranks top in the Arabian region and 32nd globally according to the International Telecommunication Union's (ITU) ICT Development Index (IDI) rankings.[36] The UAE has attained a high level of mobile-cellular penetration (over 145 % by the end of 2010) and mobile-broadband penetration (over 58 %) and a relatively high proportion of households connected to the Internet (65 %). At 78 %, it has by far the highest percentage of the population using the Internet in the region. However, both fixed-telephone penetration and fixed-broadband penetration levels remain low (~10 %) compared with other high-income economies, which effectively limits the country's ability to bring high-speed Internet access to larger parts of the population as well as to businesses and homes. Although the country has a relatively high fiber-to-the-home/business penetration rate, these subscriptions provide speeds that are below what operators in other high-income economies are now offering. In 2010, around 65 % of the UAE broadband subscriptions provided speeds of between 256 kilobytes per second and 2 megabytes per second, and 35 % speeds between 2 and 10 megabytes per second. Higher-speed subscriptions were not available. It is worth noticing that UAE is among the top 10 countries with lowest price for ICTs (Table 4.9).

In the e-government development index in United Nations E-Government Survey 2012, United Arab Emirates is especially notable as it advanced 21 positions to the ranking in 2012 of 28th globally and 5th in Asia.[37] The rapid progress of the United Arab Emirates is a best practice case highlighting how effective e-government can help support development. With double the population and three quarters of the GDP per capita, the United Arab Emirates has achieved around the same level of online services as those offered in Norway, a global leader at the eighth position.

4.2.5 Strategies

The UAE Cabinet endorsed the Federal e-government plan 2012–2014 to enhance government eServices, set up an advanced electronic infrastructure and provide an appropriate legal basis for provision of advanced eServices. These initiatives are classified into four main categories[38]:

- The legal category: includes initiatives such as creating a legal and comprehensive framework for the whole e-government project, improving the organizational structure of IT in the federal government and creating standards to define the quality of eServices.

[36] http://www.itu.int/net/pressoffice/press_releases/2012/12.aspx#.Va6VHvlVjMg

[37] http://unpan3.un.org/egovkb/Portals/egovkb/Documents/un/2012-Survey/unpan048065.pdf

[38] Government of Duibai (2012) UAE eGovernment ranked first in the Arab world and 7th worldwide in online services. e4all magazine vol. 102: 7.

Table 4.9 Internet users, population and facebook statistics for UAE, internet world stats

Country	Population (July, 2014 Est.)	Internet users (July, 2014 Est.)	Internet penetration (% population)	Facebook (31-Dec-2012)	Facebook penetration (% population)
UAE	9,445,624	8,807,226	93.24 %	3,442,940	41.7 %

	Economy	Fixed-telephone subscriptions per 100 inhabitants		Mobile-cellular subscriptions per 100 inhabitants		International Internet bandwidth Bit/s per Internet user		Percentage of households with computer		Percentage of households with Internet access	
		2011	2012	2011	2012	2011	2012	2011	2012	2011	2012
148	United Arab Emirates	23.1	24.3	148.6	169.9	24'777	36'847	77.0	85.0	67.0	72.0

	Economy	Percentage of individuals using the Internet		Fixed (wired)-broadband subscriptions per 100 inhabitants		Active mobile-broadband subscriptions per 100 inhabitants	
		2011	2012	2011	2012	2011	2012
148	United Arab Emirates	78.0	85.0	11.0	11.7	21.8	50.9

Rank	Economy	IPB		Fixed-telephone sub-basket as a % of GNI p.c.		Mobile-cellular sub-basket as a % of GNI p.c.		Fixed-broadband sub-basket as a % of GNI p.c.		GNI p.c., USD, 2011 (or latest available year)
		2012	2011	2012	2011	2012	2011	2012	2011	
7	United Arab Emirates	0.5	0.5	0.1	0.1	0.3	0.3	1.2	1.2	40'760

Top 10 in Asia

		E-gov. development index		World e-gov. development index	
Rank	Country	2014	2012	2014	2012
1	Republic of Korea	0.9462	0.9283	1	1
2	Singapore	0.9076	08474	3	10
3	Japan	0.8874	0.8019	6	18
4	Israel	0.8162	0.8100	17	16
5	Bahrain	0.8089	0.6946	18	36
6	Kazakhstan	0.7283	0.6844	28	38
7	United Arab Emirates	0.7136	0.7344	32	28
8	Saudi Arabia	0.6900	0.6658	36	41
9	Qatar	0.6362	0.6405	44	48
10	Oman	0.6273	0.5944	48	64
Regional average		0.4951	0.4992		
World average		0.4712	0.4882		

- Improving the IT Infrastructure: includes building and operating the Federal Government Information Network. It includes government call centers, data centers and disaster recovery sites in order to protect government data.
- Providing innovative applications: include the launch of the first UAEpedia, and launching of apps and eServices over mobile phones to ensure mobile on the go services.
- Effective performance management methodology: includes improving the e-government UN ranking as well as increasing customer satisfaction, building high availability policies and assurance that the government eServices will be available all the time. Moreover this category concentrates on the awareness campaigns and eServices marketing to increase user adoption.

Fig. 4.19 UAE government portal

4.2.5.1 Transparency

Most government ministries in UAE have interactive on-line presence, and a national initiative is under way to increase the number and breadth range of services available on-line.

The UAE Government recently has adopted the Open Data practice to make government data and information seamlessly available to people on the official portal of UAE government government.ae. Under the Open Data, information is made usable, reusable and accessible to the public.

By making government data and information available to the people, the UAE Government aims to create awareness among people about government statistics, reports, studies etc. resulting in enthusiastic participation from an educated and informed society.

The UAE government believes that besides enriching public participation, Open Data will also increase government transparency and the overall value the government delivers to the public (Fig. 4.19).

4.2.5.2 Practices

- **Platform Approach**

There is a so-called "platform" approach in e-government management. The platform approach does not aim at centralizing and dispatching the data but

Fig. 4.20 Abu Dhabi e-government portal

provides common tools and common functionalities (security, data exchange mechanisms, electronic signature) that allow service delivery. In this configuration, local actors are directly responsible for service provision and have to coordinate their actions (technical and organizational interoperability).

The experience of the UAE in managing its e-government initiative is instructive in this respect. While the Emirate of Dubai centrally controlled and monitored the e-services development overall, government departments were given the freedom to creatively build their own e-services in an early phase of the project. This not only accelerated development, but also helped the government departments to meet the initial target of 70 % of government services to be online by 2005.

Similarly, Dubai adopted a hybrid approach to implementing its e-government initiative whereby government departments focused on e-service enablement while the central authority focused on building common parts (e.g., payment, customer support, etc.) needed by all offices. This balance between centralization of common aspects of e-services implementation and decentralization of e-services enablement was one of the key pillars of success in the Dubai e-government initiative, which resulted in standardization, best practices sharing, cost savings, and reduced time to market.

- **Abu Dhabi e-government Portal**

The number of services provided through the Abu Dhabi e-government Portal rose to 870 from 95 government and private departments in the emirate, according to H.E. Rashid Lahej Al Mansouri, Director General of Abu Dhabi Systems and Information Center (ADSIC) (Fig. 4.20).[39]

[39] http://www.dsg.gov.ae/SiteCollectionImages/Content/DeG%20Documents/april2012_en.pdf

The portal provides a wide spectrum of services that include ID, passports, residence visas, house and land transactions, driving, travel, work, jobs, services for Emiratis religious affairs, health, safety, security, law, entertainment, culture, paying zakat, paying water and electricity bills, and pharmacies on duty.

The portal displays more than 50 online services provided by 14 government departments, and more than 800 information services provided by 95 government and semi- government departments. The portal is linked to all local and federal entities in the country.[40]

Registered users can submit enquiries, complaints or ask for information about different government department capacities and specialties. They also can view the status of their online applications through the Internet, telephone, or email.

The Abu Dhabi e-Government Portal provides a "Live Chat" service which enables registered and unregistered users to discuss their issues with customer service agents through the live communication window in the website.

- **Dubai e-government: Prosecution services on mobiles/iPads and launch of ePay service**

Dubai Public Prosecution has recently launched the case inquiry service on mobile phones as part of its efforts to invest in technology to meet its strategic objective of building a knowledge technological environment that helps upgrade work.[41] The programs target prosecution members, its HR, clients, stakeholders and the related public.

A new version of the service has been launched on the iPad under the name E-prosecutor. It will indirectly serve clients and, at the same time, will help keep the public prosecutors updated with the legal suits and cases wherever they are. Not only this, they can also take their decisions and finalize some cases which helps in faster litigation.

The Public Prosecution has also launched the UAE Laws program on the iPad with three releases in two years since the start of the project. The new release includes four laws which raise the number of laws incorporated in the system to 15 Federal Laws. In addition, the search technique has been upgraded to save users' time and efforts.

The upgraded program on the iPad allows prosecutors, lawyers, and law students to browse much more legal articles and books online instead of the traditional slow way. A new law on civil dealings has been added.

The program enables users to use their Twitter accounts and the public prosecution's Twitter accounts as well on the same screen. They can also bookmark certain materials for future reference and add their notes and comments.

Moreover, Dubai Public Prosecution has signed a memorandum of understanding with Dubai e-government to activate the ePay service in order to make it easier for clients to pay their dues and to utilize technology to save time and efforts through

---

[40] http://www.dsg.gov.ae/SiteCollectionImages/Content/DeG%20Documents/april2012_en.pdf

[41] Government of Duibai (2011) Prosecution services on mobiles/iPads and launch of ePay service with Dubai eGovernment. e4all magazine vol. 98: 3–5.

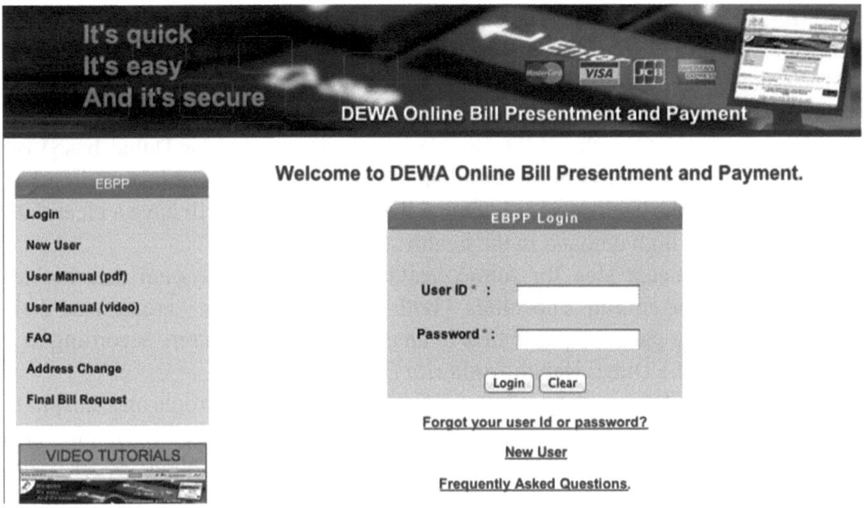

Fig. 4.21 DEWA online bill presentment and payment

paying different fees on the public prosecution's website. These include paying for applications such as requests to obtain certain certificates, delivery of passport, and civil right claims. The ePay service targets lawyers and Public Prosecution's clients who can pay easily using credit card or through direct debit from the client's bank account. Before Dubai Public Prosecution, The top three departments in terms of amounts collected were Dubai Customs, Dubai Electricity and Water Authority and the Dubai Health Authority respectively, while the top three in terms of number of transactions were DHA, DEWA and the Roads and Transport Authority respectively (Fig. 4.21).

The ePay Gateway is a centralized, integrated and secure payment gateway developed by Dubai e-government to pay for their government transactions. It has been approved by more than 20 services providers in the UAE and covers more than 200 electronic services that government departments provide to the public. The ePay system is highly secure and compliant with both Visa and MasterCard secure code programs.

- **Electronicalization of Health System in UAE**

Last year, UAE officially launched the electronic website portal for health insurance claims in the Emirate.[42] Initially this portal will capture all insurance claim arising from the Government of Dubai Employee Health insurance program known as 'Enaya' and eventually, the system will role out to all insurance plans in

[42]Anonymous (2012) Dubai Health Authority launches electronic portal for health insurance claims in the Emirate. Government of Dubai.
http://www.dha.gov.ae/EN/Media/News/Pages/DubaiHealthAuthoritylauncheselectronicportalforhealthinsuranceclaimsintheEmirate.aspx

the Emirate, which means every insurance claim in Dubai will be captured electronically.

The online system provides data about every single transaction in the health sector in the Emirate, ensuring a successful health insurance system and minimum fraud and abuse. It also offers the ability to plan clinical capacity for Dubai based on actual customer behavior patterns and data. This is also translated into an impetus for investment in the health sector in Dubai because investors will have a clear data about the areas of high demand in the health sector in Dubai.

It was a significant step for future healthcare electronic system nationwide. Almost 80 % of the emirate's hospitals – both public and private – are now on their way to transferring patients' paper files to an electronic data system, according to a recent survey by the Dubai Health Authority (DHA).

In order to switch from a paper-based filing system to an electronic one, hospitals must complete an eight-stage process in line with the Health Care Information and Management Systems Society's Electronic Medical Record Adoption Model.

A total of 23 hospitals were surveyed to see how far along they were with the process. Of those, 40 % were found to be at stage one, while a further 30 % had moved on to the second stage. Less than 10 % were on stages three and four – the highest level attained so far. To make the fourth stage, all prescriptions and doctors' orders must be inputted electronically. Others are still operating under a manual system, placing them at stage zero.

UAE will be the first country in the whole Middle East to have such a comprehensive implementation when the system is fully completed.

4.2.6 Case Study: The Russian Federation

4.2.6.1 Government Type

Russia is both a presidential and parliamentary republic.[43] The president is elected every 6 years and has certain discretionary powers which means the exclusive right of a president to make quick decisions in crisis situations when time factor is crucial (before the end of 2008 presidential term was 4 years). President serves as a referee to all power branches facilitating collaboration and conflicts resolution. The President appoints the Prime Minister who is the head of the executive administration. Legislative power is represented by two chambers: the Federal Assembly consisting of the Federation Council and State Duma (Parliament). Governors head the regional executive branches and are appointed by the President, whereas the regional legislative authorities are elected.

[43] Hohlov Y, Styrin E (2011) E-Government in Russia: Strategies of Formation and Development. In: Hohlov Y, Styrin E (ed) E-Government in Russia. IGI Global.

4.2.6.2 Infrastructure

The Russian Federation has improved its IDI value by 0.93 (around twice the global average improvement of 0.46) and moved up two places to 47th, ranking the top in CIS area. The country has improved its performance on both ICT access and use. In particular, international Internet bandwidth has increased significantly over this period on account of several submarine and transnational network infrastructure projects. For example, the operator Rostelecome doubled its Internet link capacity with Far East Telecome, up to 7.3 Gbit/s. The Russia-Japan Cable Network project was also launched, linking the two countries through an undersea cable system. Recently, Rostelecom and China Telecom announced an agreement to further expand Europe-Asia traffic, with the first phase planned to increase total capacity by 200 Gbit/s. This will serve to increase transit bandwidth in Russia for traffic between Europe and Asia through the Transit Europe-Asia (TEA) project. In the meanwhile, Internet access at home, broadband penetration and Internet usage have all increased substantially. ICT prices in the Russian Federation are lower than its income levels (Table 4.10).

In spite of the fast development, Russia's technology and connectivity infrastructure – a key enabler for adoption and use of technology – lags considerably that of Eastern Europe and developed economies.[44] The Russian government also has not yet fully leveraged online public services – including procurement – to drive technology adoption and use by Russian companies. Other major barriers to improving e-government performance include lack of appropriate skills in the workforce, and low levels of collaboration between public and private sectors.

4.2.6.3 Strategies

The e-government development strategies are embedded in this "Information Society (2011–2020)" Program, approved in October 2010. The principles of the Program could be displayed by the following five aspects[45]:

- Leadership in innovation on the basis of partnership between state, business and civil society
- Freedom and equal access to information and knowledge
- Support for domestic producers in ICT
- Programs for HRD and selection of nation- wide projects
- Promotion of international cooperation in ICT – provision of national information security

[44] Dirks S, Keeling (2009) Russia's Productivity Imperative. IBM Global Services, New York.

[45] http://www.economy.gov.ru/wps/wcm/connect/economylib4/en/home/activity/sections/infOrientedSoc/

Table 4.10 Internet users, population and Facebook statistics for Russia

Country	Population (July, 2014 Est.)	Internet users (July, 2014 Est.)	Internet penetration (% population)	Facebook (31-Dec-2012)	Facebook penetration (% population)
Russian Federation	142,467,651	84,437,793	59.27 %	7,963,400	5.6 %

	Economy	Fixed-telephone subscriptions per 100 inhabitants 2011	2012	Mobile-cellular subscriptions per 100 inhabitants 2011	2012	International Internet bandwidth Bit/s per Internet user 2011	2012	Percentage of households with computer 2011	2012	Percentage of households with Internet access 2011	2012
118	Russian Federation	30.9	30.1	179.3	183.5	31'911	32'945	57.1	60.6	46.0	51.2

	Economy	Percentage of individuals using the Internet 2011	2012	Fixed (wired)-broadband subscriptions per 100 inhabitants 2011	2012	Active mobile-broadband subscriptions per 100 inhabitants 2011	2012
118	Russian Federation	49.0	53.3	12.2	14.5	48.0	53.0

Rank	Economy	IPB 2012	2011	Fixed-telephone sub-basket as a % of GNI p.c. 2012	2011	Mobile-cellular sub-basket as a % of GNI p.c. 2012	2011	Fixed-broadband sub-basket as a % of GNI p.c. 2012	2011	GNI p.c., USD, 2011 (or latest available year)
23	Russian Federation	1.0	1.0	0.5	0.8	1.3	1.1	1.2	1.2	10'400

Top 10 in Eastern Europe

		E-gov. development index		World e-gov. development index	
RANK	COUNTRY	2014	2012	2014	2012
1	Russian Federation	0.7296	0.7345	27	27
2	Hungary	0.6637	0.7201	39	31
3	Poland	0.6482	0.6441	42	47
4	Solvakia	0.6148	0.6292	51	53
5	Czech Republic	0.6070	0.6491	53	46
6	Belarus	0.6053	0.6090	55	61
7	Romania	0.5632	0.6060	64	62
8	Republic of Moldova	0.5571	0.5626	66	69
9	Bulgaria	0.5421	0.6132	73	60
10	Ukraine	0.5032	0.5653	87	68
Regional average		0.6034	0.6333		
World average		0.4712	0.4882		

Source: Internet world stats

The objectives of the formation of the Russian Federation e-government are[46]:

- to improve the quality and accessibility of public services for organizations and citizens, simplifying procedures and reducing the time of their delivery, reducing administrative costs for citizens and entities obtaining government services, as well as the introduction of uniform standards of services to citizens;
- to enhance the transparency of information about the activities of government bodies and to expand the ability to access it and to enhance direct participation

[46]ADOC 2.0 Workshop 2011 (2011) Tracking Digital Divide: Russia's Policies and Priorities. Apecdoc. http://www.apecdoc.org/site/adocsecretariat/files/2011/08/07-26下午場7-Presentation_Russia.pdf

of organizations, citizens and civil society institutions in the procedures of formation and examination of the decisions taken at all levels of government;
- to improve the quality of administrative and management processes;
- to improve information and analytical support for decision making at all levels of government so as to ensure prompt and complete control over the effectiveness of the activities of government bodies and to provide the required level of security of e-government in its functioning.

Moreover, by July 1, 2012 all regions and municipalities of Russia will go to the electronic inter-agency cooperation. This was announced by Prime Minister Vladimir Putin, speaking in the Duma in 2011. Rostelecom will connect 70 regions of Russia to a single system of e-government while leaving 13 regions developing their own regional versions.[47]

4.2.6.4 Transparency

Russia's e-government project took off in April 2010.[48, 49] The project is aimed at taking care of Russians' day-to-day bureaucracy on-line, as well as at turning the country into an information society. Although President Medvedev promised that by 2015 all Russian government forms will be completed online and many e-government advances have been made recently, the transparency in Russian's governments is far from satisfying.[50]

The Freedom of Information Act has been passed by Duma and in effect since 2010. It's a big momentum on Russia's way to changing the whole system into being open and transparent. Its implementation is lacking, however. Little if any information is provided when requests are put to authorities. Many courts were unwilling to publish short bios and pictures of their judges online Very few government agencies, federal or regional, want their financial records in public view. Information on cash flow, which could expose corruption, is kept secret – not only by the authorities, but by non-profit organizations as well.

Founded in 2004, the non-profit organization Freedom of Information Foundation (FIF) kept studying compliance of contents of governmental and local

---

[47] Anonymous (2012) Rostelekom Oao: 70 Russian Regions Connected To Russia's E-Government System By Rostelecom. 4-Traders. http://www.4-traders.com/ROSTELEKOM-OAO-6491738/news/Rostelekom-OAO-70-RUSSIAN-REGIONS-CONNECTED-TO-RUSSIA-S-E-GOVERNMENT-SYSTEM-BY-ROSTELECOM-14274272/

[48] Carlsson SH (2012) Russia: The Early Days of Government Transparency. Global Voice. http://globalvoicesonline.org/2012/03/01/russia-the-early-days-of-government-transparency/

[49] Sidorenko A (2011) Russia: E-Gov Blogger Discusses Technology and Transparency (Video). Global Voice. http://globalvoicesonline.org/2011/05/04/russia-e-gov-blogger-discusses-technology-and-transparency-video/

[50] Anonymous (2012) Divorce at a Click: Russia Brings in e-Government. UNPAN. http://www.unpan.org/PublicAdministrationNews/tabid/116/mctl/ArticleView/ModuleID/1469/articleId/30371/default.aspx

Table 4.11 Summary statistics for informational openness growth rates among monitored entities

Monitoring cycle	Totally sites	EXMO totally	EXMO active	Rate growth for all	Rate growth for active	Communication duration
Top executive government bodies of the Russian Federation subjects	83	25	13	1.5 %	27 %	4 weeks
General jurisdiction courts	2379	468	127	2.54 %	47.75 %	4 weeks
Arbitration courts	112	51	31	6.69 %	28.08 %	1 month
Judicial Department bodies	85	55	27	13.736 %	35.005 %	6 weeks
Community foundations	18	12	5	3.852 %	13.867 %	3 weeks

self-government bodies' official websites with actual legislation and with information users' needs. The summary statistic data (Table 4.11) for 2011 monitoring results displays obvious and limited growth of government websites' informational openness.[51] where

- "EXMO Totally" column shows number of entities whose representatives registered for communication in EXMO though not all of them really took part in the online dialog with our experts;
- "EXMO Active" column shows how many number of entities whose representatives took real part in communication by means of making at least one comment in EXMO;
- "Rate Growth for All" column shows average informational openness rate growth during the monitoring period over all entities monitored within each specific cycle;
- "Rate Growth for Active" column shows average informational openness rate growth during the monitoring period over entities whose representatives took real part in communication.

Let's take the example of E-Russia program. One of its goals was to provide harmonious entry of Russia into the world economy through cooperation and information transparency. However the $220 M program funds during 2002–2005 actually did relatively little to broaden the geography and demographics of Internet access. The bulk of the funds were allocated towards enhancing the networking infrastructure and building up information systems only within governmental organizations. Since the Internet is oriented towards the political elite, the level of the information transparency that is being provided can only be very limited.[52]

[51] Freedom of Information Foundation (2011) Annual Report 2011. Svobodainfo. http://www.svobodainfo.org/en/node/1677

[52] McHenry W, Borisov A (2006) E-Government And Democracy In Russia. Communications of the Association for Information Systems 17: 1064–1123

Another fact worth noting in Russia's political governance is its notorious corruption. Despite President Dmitry Medvedev's efforts to fight corruption, its level remains extremely high, with the country ranking 143rd out of 182 countries in Transparency International's 2011 Corruption Perceptions Index. Transparency construction through e-government should be one of the antidotes. Government information must be available so that the public can exercise control over it and oversee its actions. Despite Russian President Dmitry Medvedev's efforts to fight corruption, its level in Russia remains extremely high, with the country ranking 133rd out of 176 countries in Transparency International's 2012 Corruption Perceptions Index.[53] Russia's ranking indicates an improvement on its 154th place in the Berlin-based anti-corruption watchdog's 2010 list.

4.2.6.5 Practices

- **Services 2.0 – New Version E-Government Portal**[54]

Last year, the new version of Russian e-government portal Gosuslugi.ru was launched by the state-controlled telecoms giant Rostelecom, officially the only telecommunications company permitted to create infrastructure for the country's electronic government service (Fig. 4.22).

Some eye-catching features of the new, rebranded "state services 2.0" version of the web site include:

- It is available on all platforms – personal and tablet computers and smartphones, including devices with sensory screens.
- State services will be accessible via special terminals, or "infomats" (also called "electronic public servants" by the Russian media), 500 of which will be installed across Russia by 2015.
- The new, more user-friendly interface and the slogan "State services – transparent as ever!"
- It allows its 752,583 account holders to use it for a number of operations: from paying taxes and registering a car to getting a passport.

Problems persist, however. The Russian Internet has abundant negative comments regarding the speed at which the web site loads, the quality of its performance and numerous errors. A typical example is a woman who tried to reserve a spot in a kindergarten for her son through the portal and discovered that he needs a passport and a pension insurance certificate – both issued in adulthood.

[53] Transparency International (2012) Corruption Perceptions Index 2012. Transparency International, Berlin.

[54] Razumovskaya O (2011) New Governmental Portal Starts. The Moscow Times. http://www.themoscowtimes.com/business/article/new-e-government-portal-starts/436563.html

Fig. 4.22 The Russian Federation government portal

- **Rosreestr – Federal Service of State Registration Cadastre and Mapping of Russia**[55]

Russia is the largest country in the world, covering more than a ninth of the earth's land area. Spanning nine time zones, it is home to 143 million people. Managing the property rights for so many across this vast landscape is a monumental task.

Until a few years ago, Russian property rights, cadastre, and mapping were managed by separate agencies. This meant that while the Russian cadastre was completely mapped and recorded, the data was not consolidated. Changes in legislation to improve public-oriented services led to merging these functions. A federal law was adopted requiring the country's cadastre information to be made accessible to the general public over the Internet in the form of maps. Displaying cadastral information in this form would make the information easier to understand by the people who need it.

Today, legislative and regulatory issues related to cadastral matters are managed by one agency, the Ministry of Economic Development. A public geoportal run by the Federal Service of State Registration Cadastre and Mapping of Russia (Rosreestr) (maps.rosreestr.ru/portal) now stores and delivers Russian cadastral

[55] Ushakov A (2011) Federal Geoportal Provides Access to Cadastral Information. ESRI. http://www.esri.com/news/arcnews/fall11articles/russia-introduces-e-government.html

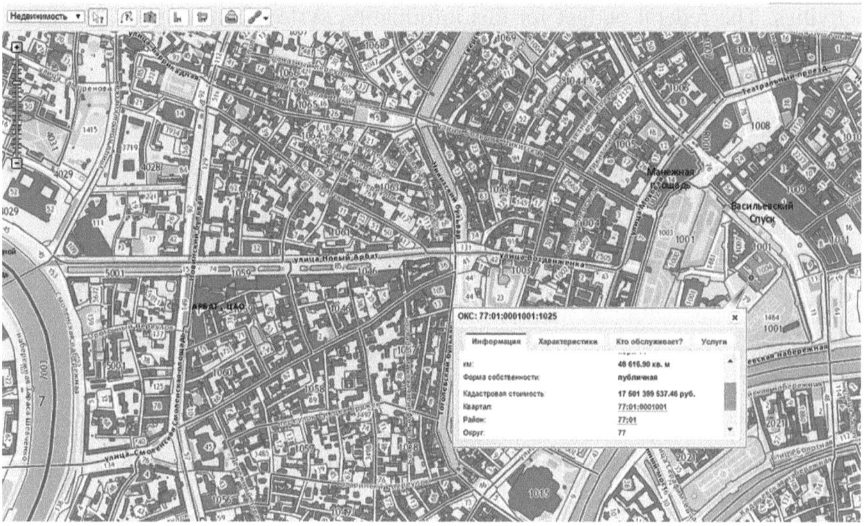

Fig. 4.23 Rosreestr

data. Data comes from the Federal Real Estate Cadastre and includes information for registration of rights, receipt of information, and documentation. The geoportal provides the means for anyone to access unclassified data for the entire country quickly and reliably. Using the site, Russian citizens can receive real estate documents more quickly and cheaply than by standing in line at the government agency to request information, then waiting for their documents to be sent via post (Fig. 4.23).

The Ministry of Economic Development, which promotes housing development, greenfield urbanization, and support of future growth, is finding that the portal is speeding up the receipt of necessary legal documents. The time frame for obtaining cadastre certificates and registration of land plots has been greatly reduced by having information consolidated and put into a uniform format.

The portal offers several state services – both at no cost and for a fee – through the public cadastre maps. Free public reference services include the ability to find and map the parcel cadastre number and address, land status, parcel area, land-use category, assessed value of the parcel or property, parcel or property statements for reference purposes, and contact information of a local land administration.

- **Implementation of IT system for the Ministry of Health**

Ministry of Health began monitoring the pilot areas for the introduction of a unified medical IT system in April 2012. It will introduce electronic cards to patients, provide remote consultations, as well as electronicalize the management of clinic activities. The federal budget for this information system is as high as 29 billion Rubles.[56] By July 2012 in pilot areas a number of basic services will be tested:

For internal use of physicians:

- System of user identification
- Email exchange services
- Administrative management (accounting, personnel, etc.)
- Medical insurance payment
- Information and analytical decision support subsystem (service EAC)

For external use of patients:

- Integrated electronic medical records (IEMK),
- Schedules management
- Medical consultation and telemedicine

Duplication of the system the whole federation is scheduled to be completed before the end of 2012.

- **E-Education**[57]

In February 2012, President Dmitry Medvedev legalized the E-Learning program that requires educational institutions to offer distance education programs.

Education on the Internet has exited in universities and technical schools of Russia for a while, but it was actually outside the legal field. Now this electronic program received official status. The program imposed more stringent requirements for institutions that offer electronic education: availability of specific e-books, textbooks, facilities and general information infrastructure, which means some unqualified education institutions – with no electronic textbooks, educational environment, databases, and most importantly, no specially trained teachers and administrators would be out in the market. Especially universities engaging in e-learning will be required to rewrite the textbooks in accordance with international standards.

In the meantime, in March 2012, Togliatti Library received funding of 4.6 million Rubles, which will be used to build 25 electronic rooms for children equipped with modern computers and information technologies, and to upgraded information system and network within its 26 branch libraries and 10 centers. The Department of Culture hopes this will become a legacy in the following electronicalization of learning and education. One disadvantage is that the budget for the program did not include material stimulation of staff in libraries.

- **Sberbank provided a connection to СМЭВ**[58]

---

[56] Legeza D (2012). ИТ-система Минздрава за 29 млрд рублей: как стартовало внедрение. CNews. http://www.cnews.ru/news/top/index.shtml?2012/04/13/485703

[57] Ivoilova I (2012) Медведев узаконил электронное обучение. RG. http://www.rg.ru/2012/02/29/obrazovanie-site.html

[58] Anonymous (2012) ФНС России подвела первые итоги работы СМЭВ. CNews. http://corp.cnews.ru/news/line/index.shtml?2012/01/10/471935

On April 5 2012, Sberbank entered into commercial operation on payment service of tax through on the site for its client. Sberbank was also the first commercial financial institution connected to the government's interagency cooperation system (СМЭВ).

In the past, citizens had to log on to the website of the Federal Tax Service (FTS) (nalog.ru), typed into their taxpayer identification number (TIN), and then pay through link of Sberbank. So connecting to СМЭВ avoided the redundancy for Sberbank to exchange data with different departments separately. The services will be available through ATMs and terminals of the bank soon. Mobilization is also Sberbank's plan for next step: client of the bank will be notified of tax due and make the payment by just pressing a single button on their mobile phone.

In the near future, Sberbank intends to expand personal payment services into traffic police fines, passports and Federal Prosecution service.

At the same time, the Federal Treasury has signed agreement with about 30 banks, including Bank of Moscow, Gazprombank and QIWI bank for building such convenient and efficient electronic payment system.

In 2013 a similar connection to СМЭВ will be required for all companies wishing to make payments to state agencies.

4.2.7 Case Study: Mauritius

4.2.7.1 Government Type

Politics of Mauritius takes place in a framework of a parliamentary representative democratic republic, in which the President is the head of state and the prime minister is the head of government who is assisted by a council of Ministers. Mauritius has a multi-party system. Executive power is exercised by the government. Legislative power is vested in both the government and the National Assembly. The absolute power is split between two positions: the President and the Prime Minister.[59]

Infrastructure

Mauritius is the highest ranked country in Africa in terms of IDI, but only 69th place globally. Progress in Mauritius was driven by strong increases in the number of active mobile-broadband subscriptions and it has achieved mobile-broadband penetration rates of above 15 % and broadband penetration rate above 1 %. In many African countries, hardly any rural inhabitants were using Internet in 2007–2008, but Mauritius even achieved Internet usage among rural individuals of 21.9 %. ICT prices are lower than the income level in Mauritius (Table 4.12).

[59] http://en.wikipedia.org/wiki/Mauritius

Table 4.12 Internet users, population and Facebook statistics for Mauritius, internet live stats

Country	Population (July, 2014 Est.)	Internet users (July, 2014 Est.)	Internet penetration (% population)	Facebook (31-Dec-2012)	Facebook penetration (% population)
Mauritius	1,249,151	76,681	6.14 %	367,900	28.0 %

	Economy	Fixed-telephone subscriptions per 100 inhabitants 2011	Fixed-telephone subscriptions per 100 inhabitants 2012	Mobile-cellular subscriptions per 100 inhabitants 2011	Mobile-cellular subscriptions per 100 inhabitants 2012	International Internet bandwidth Bit/s per Internet user 2011	International Internet bandwidth Bit/s per Internet user 2012	Percentage of households with computer 2011	Percentage of households with computer 2012	Percentage of households with Internet access 2011	Percentage of households with Internet access 2012
94	Mauritius	28.7	26.6	99.0	113.1	12'714	14'613	38.2	40.6	36.4	42.0

	Economy	Percentage of individuals using the Internet 2011	Percentage of individuals using the Internet 2012	Fixed (wired)-broadband subscriptions per 100 inhabitants 2011	Fixed (wired)-broadband subscriptions per 100 inhabitants 2012	Active mobile-broadband subscriptions per 100 inhabitants 2011	Active mobile-broadband subscriptions per 100 inhabitants 2012
94	Mauritius	35.0	41.4	9.8	10.6	12.6	21.7

Rank	Economy	IPB 2012	IPB 2011	Fixed-telephone sub-basket as a % of GNI p.c. 2012	Fixed-telephone sub-basket as a % of GNI p.c. 2011	Mobile-cellular sub-basket as a % of GNI p.c. 2012	Mobile-cellular sub-basket as a % of GNI p.c. 2011	Fixed-broadband sub-basket as a % of GNI p.c. 2012	Fixed-broadband sub-basket as a % of GNI p.c. 2011	GNI p.c., USD, 2011 (or latest available year)
35	Mauritius	1.2	1.3	0.8	0.8	0.9	1.0	1.8	2.0	8'240

Top 10 in Africa

		E-gov. development index		World e-gov. development index	
Rank	Country	2014	2012	2014	2012
1	Tunisia	0.5390	0.4833	75	103
2	Mauritius	0.5338	0.5066	76	93
3	Egypt	0.5129	0.4611	80	107
4	Seychelles	0.5113	0.5192	81	84
5	Morocco	0.5060	0.4209	82	120
6	South Africa	0.4869	0.4869	93	101
7	Botswana	0.4198	0.4186	112	121
8	Narmibia	0.3880	0.3937	117	123
9	Kenya	0.3805	0.4212	119	119
10	Libya	0.3753	N/A	121	191
Regional average		0.2661	0.2780		
World average		0.4712	0.4882		

In spite of the encouraging progress made so far, a number of challenges have been identified such as human resources, fund constraints, technical back up support and above all an absence of ownership of these projects at departmental levels in the development of ICT in Mauritius.

Strategies

National Information & Communication Technology Strategic Plan (NICTSP) 2007–2011 clearly indicated that Mauritius required comprehensive process re-engineering and coordinated planning to deliver citizen-centric services. It envisaged a systematic marketing of e-Government as a tool for good governance covering aspects of efficiency, accountability and transparency.

The latest NICTSP 2011–2014: Towards i-Mauritius[60] outlined visions and measures to:

- Continue make the ICT sector one of the main pillars of the economy and transforming Mauritius into a regional ICT hub.
- Position Mauritius as a preferred ICT destination both regionally and globally as well as to make of the Internet a basic citizen right and build an inclusive information society.
- Provide 24/7 e-Government services.
- Develop and implement a comprehensive cyber security strategy.

Specifically, in the e-government area, Mauritius hopes to achieve in the following two aspects:

- Refine the strategic areas for e-Government services based on user needs, including the preparation for e-Government Apex Body plan, launch of Mauritius National Identity Card (MNIC) plans and the strengthening of Data Protection in e-government
- Build an e-Government brand for Mauritius and strengthening the sectoral champions, including national e-Government needs survey on citizen and business centric services and implementation of e-Gov Brand Marketing and Awareness Campaign

4.2.7.2 Transparency

Since 1996, Mauritius has been putting all ministries online with web sites containing information about their work, including legal texts, publications, events and services available to the public and contact details. Nowadays, public administration web sites – including the 26 ministries and over 80 governmental bodies – are linked through the Government of Mauritius web portal (www.gov.mu). Until 2005, all government services have been put online.

However, as pointed in the NICTSP 2011–2014, a number of projects aimed at e-Government and service delivery to the citizens during 2007–2011 were more sporadic and did not systematically follow the flow chain and priorities set by the NICTSP. The computerization process of civil service or government offices is sometimes perceived a procurement and installation than a means to deliver the need-based services to the citizens.

The next step for the improvement of e-government services in Mauritius involves making the transition from static web sites to fully integrated transactional services. E-Government would be accessible from a variety of access points including traditional counter services, as well as the Internet, kiosks and call centers.

[60] Gillwald A, Islam B (2011) National Information & Communication Technology Strategic Plan (Nictsp) 2011–2014: Towards I-Mauritius. Ministry of Information and Communication Technology. http://mtci.govmu.org/English//DOCUMENTS/NICTSP20112014.PDF

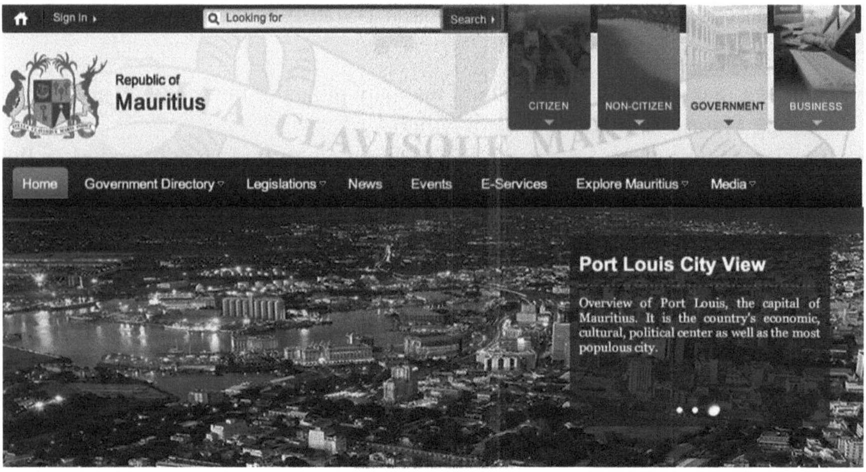

Fig. 4.24 Mauritius government portal

Transparency will continuously be one of the objectives in Mauritius' e-government development plan, and future national e-government survey across the nation would further identify the most sought after services that the users would like to have online in terms of easy access, transparency, and cost-effectiveness.

4.2.7.3 Practices

- **Government Online Centre**[61]

The Government Online Centre hosts the government web portal, which is the single window to deliver integrated services to citizens, non-citizens, government and business. It enables the government to bring together services and organize them in a way that is convenient and logical for users. By delivering services in this way, citizens and businesses no longer need to understand how the government system is organized or which department is responsible for specific services from the government or which departments the citizen or user needs to interact with, for a particular government service (Fig. 4.24).

The "Citizen" portion of Mauritius' integrated portal is organized primarily around key services, but also groups information by audience and includes an A–Z thematic index. Additional features that aid the citizen in quickly finding content include a "Quick Links" box, a "Related Subject Areas" box, and a government directory. The directory can be displayed according to hierarchy or in alphabetical order by ministry or department name.

[61] Ramessur TS (2009) E-Governance and Online Public Service: The Case of a Cyber Island. International Journal of Computing and ICT Research, Vol. 3, No. 2: 12–19. http://www.ijcir.org/volume3-number2/article2.pdf

GOC houses the following fully online and interactive e-Services:

- Application for scholarship
- Application for driving licenses
- Application for work permits
- Application for vacancies published by the Public Service Commission
- Application for Lump Sums

The GOC is hosting some 175 websites including Ministries, Departments and Parastatal bodies -an increase from only 86 websites in 2005. Applications submitted online for e-services (some even prior to the NICTSP) like Learner's Driving Licenses have increased from 1,868 in 2005 to 32,149 in 2009. Likewise, applications for public vacancies at the Public Service Commission through e-forms have also increased, from only 448 applications in 2005 to 3,159 in 2009. Further, electronic submission of tax returns (both individual and business) has also increased considerably.

Government Online Centre (GOC) is in the heart of past e-service. A tender for Phase I was launched in January 2003. This phase developed an E-Centre and Government Portal. Phase II of the project focuses on disaster recovery and Phase III is to build a Government Call Centre to handle queries.

- **Universal ICT Education Program (UIEP)**[62]

This program, approved in March 2006, aims at imparting computer proficiency skills to all students, workers, unemployed people, and the population at large. Through the UIEP, the government is aiming to train 400,000 trainees over 4 years to obtain the internationally recognized Internet and Computing Core Certification (IC3). This program would create a significant pool of ICT professionals, which, in turn, would attract employers interested in using Mauritius as an ICT bridge between India and Africa and between India and French-speaking countries. The main objectives of UIEP are to:

- Make an e-society where ICT pervades all spheres of social development and well- being of all Mauritians
- Meet the demand of ICT manpower for the industry
- Align Mauritius to international benchmarking in ICT literacy
- Encourage people to go for higher-level industry-based certifications

The program delivers an IC3 basic computing skills course in 59 training centers that are situated in schools across Mauritius. The Internet and Computing Core Certification was developed by Certiport Incorporation (US) and is the first globally accepted, standards-based, validated certification program for basic computing skills. Becoming IC3 certified demonstrates that one possesses the knowledge required for basic use of computer hardware, software, and the Internet, which are nowadays prerequisites for virtually every placement opportunity.

[62] Issacs S (2007) ICT in Education in Mauritius. InfoDev. www.infodev.org/ict4edu-Africa

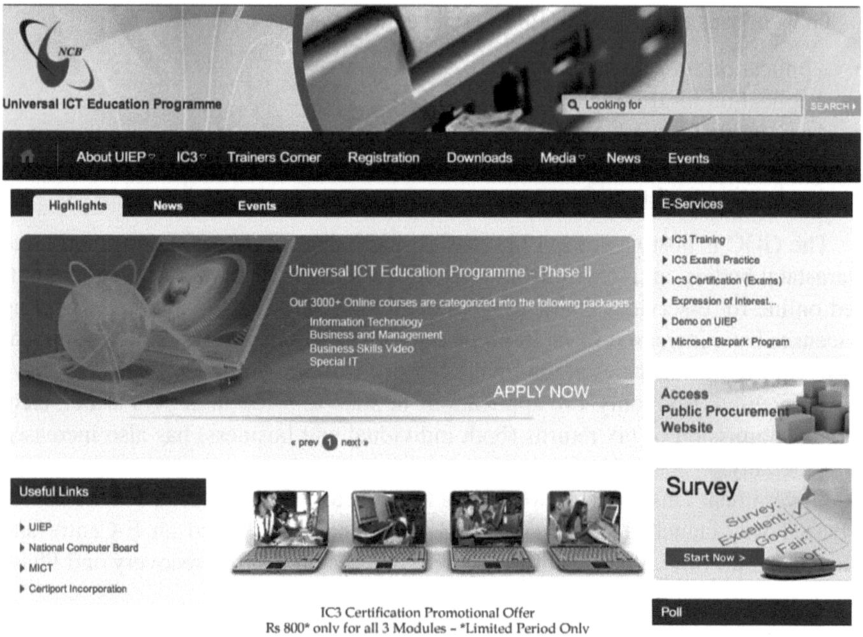

Fig. 4.25 Universal ICT education program

Mauritians who successfully obtain the IC3 certification under UIEP will be able to follow professional ICT courses at a 95 % discounted rate. The UIEP aims at imparting computer proficiency skills to over 400,000 persons over the next 4 years (Fig. 4.25).

- **E-taxation**

The integration of government processes to achieve enhanced service delivery has been adopted in Mauritius since 2000. The joint public and private sector Contributions Network Project (CNP) connects all large firms, and the majority of small ones, to the relevant government tax departments via a single channel for electronic submission of payments such as contributions, tax returns, etc. that Mauritian firms make to various government departments. Initiated by the Ministry of Finance, the system enables employers to submit their returns directly through a two-way, fully electronic system. In return, employers receive confirmations from the respective departments. Payments are also made electronically through a direct debit arrangement. The payments covered under the project include PAYE (Pay As You Earn), Corporate Income Tax, VAT (Value Added Tax), NPS (National Pensions Scheme), NSF (National Savings Fund), the IVTB levy and company registration.

It is clear that the adoption of this electronic lodgment system promises multiple advantages:

- Allows submission from the comfort of one's office with a PC and modem
- Eliminates paper returns and paper payments

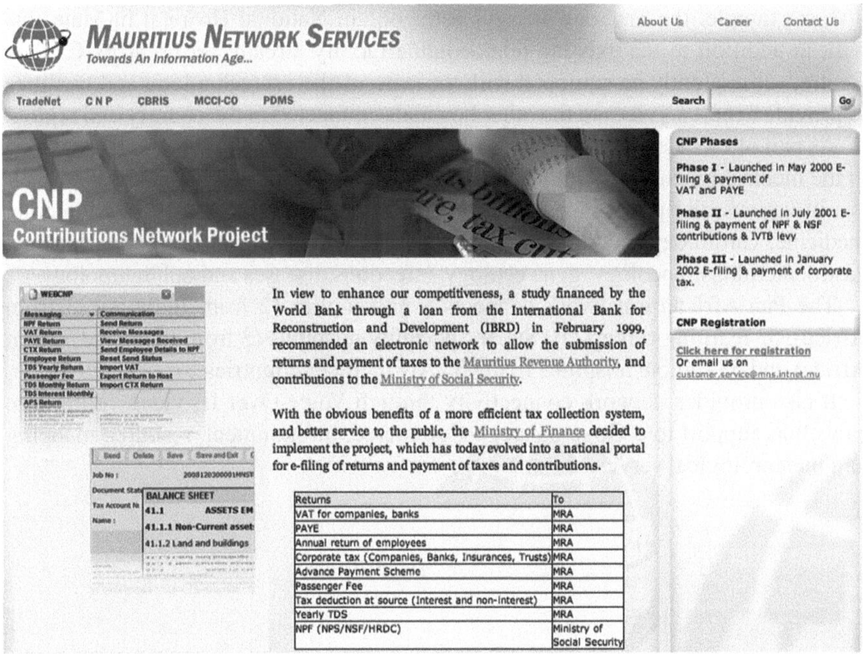

Fig. 4.26 Mauritius network services

Fig. 4.27 The pan-African e-network project

- No physical movement required to the Government departments
- Saves time and increases efficiency for businesses/employers and Government
- Guarantees confidentiality and security (Fig. 4.26)

- **The Pan African e-Network Project**[63]

In 2009 Mauritius was selected to host the 'Super Speciality' Regional Hospital of the Pan African e-Network Project.

The Pan African e-Network Project, meant to connect 53 countries of the African Union (AU) by satellite and fiber optic network, is an initiative of the former President of India P.J. Abdul Kalam. This project aims to create significant linkages for tele-education and tele-medicine, making available the facilities and expertise of some of the best universities and Super Speciality hospitals in India to the people of Africa (Fig. 4.27).

[63]Anonymous (2009) Mauritius to host Pan African 'Super Speciality' Hospital. IFG. http://www.ifg.cc/index.php?option=com_content&task=view&id=27958&Itemid=1

For example, the Sir Seewoosagur Ramgoolam National Hospital in Mauritius will, in addition to the existing telemedicine facility already set up at its Cardiac Centre, subsequently be equipped with the state-of-the-art technology and facilities to provide expert services to the other hospitals connected in the country and region.

As part of the tele-medicine services, online medical consultation will be provided to the medical practitioners in the patient-end locations from Indian medical specialists in various disciplines, specialities and sub-specialities, such as general/internal medicine, cardiology, neurology, pathology, dermatology, urology, endocrinology, gastroenterology, oncology, gyna ecology, infectious diseases and ophthalmology.

The Pan African e-network connects 5 universities (2 from India and 3 from Africa), 53 learning centers, 10 Super Speciality hospitals (3 from India and 7 from Africa) and 53 remote hospitals in the 53 AU member countries.

It also provides network connectivity through Voice-Over IP, video conference as well as support to e-Governance, e-Commerce, infotainment, resource mapping and meteorological services.

Chapter 5
Conclusion

This process isn't something government can do alone – you need to play your part too. Use this information, exploit it, hold your public services to account. They are there for you, so make them work for you.

– Prime Minister David Cameron, United Kingdom

All three levels or stages can be found in the UN's four stages of e-government development. Ultimately, government should strive for level three as it is the only sustainable level. In recent months, many governments have experienced the impact of the latest global oil and gas crisis, they have set new national energy strategies, looking at alternative sources and technologies. There is a very close relationship with e-government and its sustainable future. If government can manage its resources better by understanding the needs and making decisions based on intelligent analysis, it can create a sustainable environment for citizens.

At level one, it is not sustainable as it is not looking at the long-term plan for the country and its citizens. At level two, it is still not sustainable as the government has no clear strategy for future sustainability and its interest lies with current social, economic, and political demand. For example, all governments should mandate a paperless business approach and adopt an e-document system. This type of mandate has a major impact on all levels of society especially the private sector. In the long run, it is a sustainable approach to the system.

Given how ICTs have changed the world in a short time period, achievement of level three appears inevitable. The rapidly changing ICT world, technologies like Web 2.0, which made the digital world more participatory, and the current "Milleniels" generation expects to play an active role in all aspects of society. In fact these new technologies are part of the next generation of Web or Web 3.0, which will be a smarter web that will seamlessly orchestrate all data around the world and cross wire and wireless devices and platforms.

In order to achieve the level three e-governments, government must consider the following (Fig. 5.1):

- It should have a clear national strategy or roadmap on sustainable e-government. This strategy should be clearly mapped to the resources and environment.

D. Anderson et al., *E-Government Strategy, ICT and Innovation for Citizen Engagement*, SpringerBriefs in Electrical and Computer Engineering,
DOI 10.1007/978-1-4939-3350-1_5

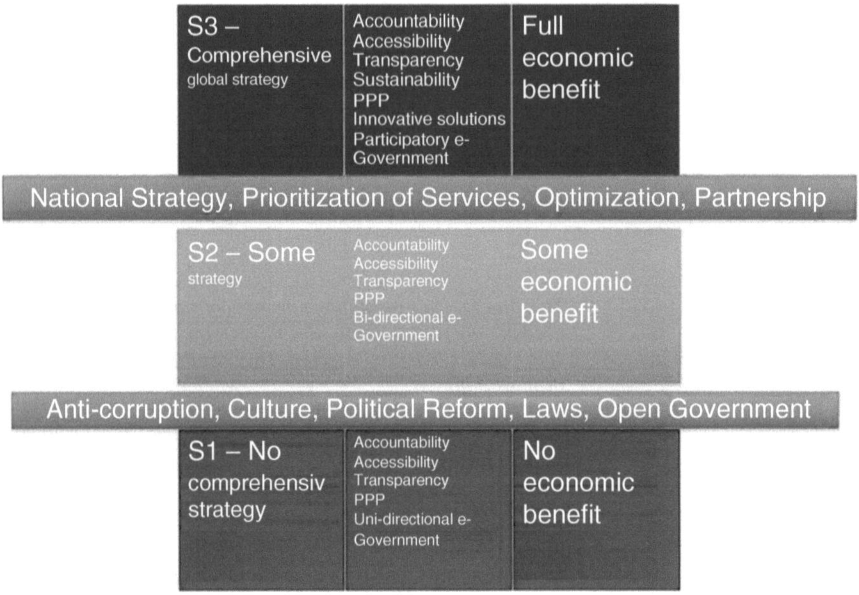

Fig. 5.1 Three levels in e-government and requirements

The national strategy should be based on (1) a census that can provide clear demographic information such as ethnicity, income, gender, age, language, household size, etc., a top-down government review of services and functions, and a budget allocation; (2) after collecting the basic information aforementioned, it should do a SWOT (Strength, Weakness, Opportunities, and Threats) analysis. There should be multi-level SWOT analysis (i.e., top to bottom inter and intra governmental review, local government need assessment, national commission, citizens groups, etc.) and a consolidation of analysis and set goals and objectives. The process should include local governments as many citizens are more familiar with their community and local needs (Fig. 5.2). This is particularly important for MDGs. A key to achieving many MDGs depends on how well the national strategy is directly mapped to the local communities where the real needs are and bring necessary resources to address problems like extreme poverty, poor health care, lack of education, etc.; (3) at the same time, develop a national sustainability strategy and map the e-government strategy to its goals.

- It must have a legal and technical framework to support the e-government initiatives.
- It should dedicate sufficient budget to support the e-government initiatives.
- It should deploy technologies to provide accessibility to all citizens, i.e., wireless technologies and m-government applications for people with disability and senior citizens.
- It should mandate all government units to have goals and objectives for e-government.

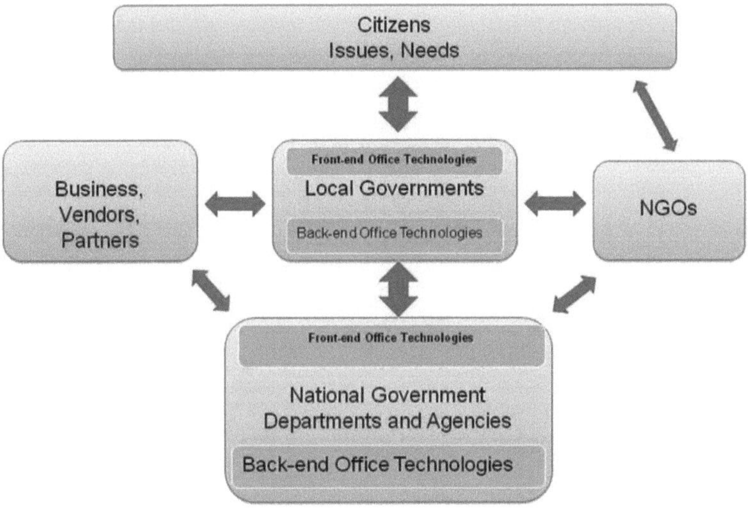

Fig. 5.2 Connecting the national government e-government to the local entities

- It should create educational and training programs for current and future government employees. It should also find ways to recruit and retain knowledge workers and leaders.
- There should be a presidential-level commission to integrate all government branches and units. This commission should include citizen organizations and the private sector.
- It must be open to citizen participation. This should be the core of e-government.
- Create a mechanism to promote public-private partnerships to ensure that the e-government initiative promotes economic growth (i.e., jobs, new businesses and technologies).
- There should be transparent assessment and evaluation throughout the system (i.e., procurements, grants, budget spending, etc.).

A sustainable e-government knows what the citizens need, based on citizen participation and properly distributing its resources while managing and creating sustainable resources.

References

Alberti, A., & Klareskov, V. (2006). *Innovations in governance and public administration: Replicating what works*. New York: United Nations. Print.

Anderson, D., & Cho, J. (2010). *The role of public service in achieving the millennium development goals*. Retrieved July 27, 2015, from http://unpan1.un.org/intradoc/groups/public/documents/un-dpadm/unpan039238.pdf

Ardıç, N. (2012). Understanding the 'Arab Spring': Justice, dignity, religion and international politics. *Afro Eurasian Studies, 1*(1), 8–52.

Bertot, J., Jaeger, P., & Grimes, J. (2010). Using ICTs to create a culture of transparency: E-government and social media as openness and anti-corruption tools for societies. *Government Information Quarterly, 27*, 264–271.

Boonmee, J. (1999). The true cost of Y2K. *Smart Computing, 7*(8), 3.

Chen, A., Pan, S., Zhang, J., Huang, W., & Zhu, S. (n.d.). Managing e-government implementation in China: A process perspective. *Information & Management, 46*(4), 203–212.

Cho, J., & Soon, A. (2010). Ubiquitous government: mobile portal for Seoul Metropolitan Government. *Proceedings of the 11th annual international digital government research conference on public administration online: Challenges and opportunities* (pp. 247–248). Digital Government Society of North America.

Davison, R., Wagner, C., & Ma, L. (2005). From government to e-government: A transition model. *Information Technology & People Info Technology & People, 18*(3), 280–299.

Dawes, S. (2008). The evolution and continuing challenges of e-governance. *Public Administration Review, 68*(s1), S86–S102.

Division for Public Administration and Development Management (DPADM). (2012). Retrieved July 27, 2015, from http://www.unpan.org/DPADM/MajorPublications/UNEGovernmentSurvey/EGovernmentReadinessKnowledgeBaseUNKB/tabid/718/Default.aspx

European Commission. (2007, September). The user challenge. Benchmarking the supply of online public services. Retrieved July 27, 2015, from http://ec.europa.eu/atoz_en.htm

Fang, Z. (2002). E-government in digital era: Concept, practice, and development. *International Journal of The Computer, The Internet and Management, 10*(2), 1–22.

Fountain, J. (2001). *Building the virtual state information technology and institutional change*. Washington, DC: Brookings Institution Press.

Frieden, R. (2005). Lessons from broadband development in Canada, Japan, Korea and the United States. *Telecommunications Policy, 29*, 595–613.

Fu, Y., & Xiao, K. (2012). Software engineering and service science (ICSESS), 2012. *IEEE 3rd international conference. Promoting sustainable e-government with multichannel service*

D. Anderson et al., *E-Government Strategy, ICT and Innovation for Citizen Engagement*, SpringerBriefs in Electrical and Computer Engineering,
DOI 10.1007/978-1-4939-3350-1

delivery: A case study. http://ieeexplore.ieee.org/xpl/login.jsp?tp=&arnumber=6269561&url=http%3A%2F%2Fieeexplore.ieee.org%2Fxpls%2Fabs_all.jsp%3Farnumber%3D6269561

Gant, D., Gant, J., & Johnson, C. (2002). *State web portals: Delivering and financing e-service*. Arlington, VA: The PricewaterhouseCoopers Endowment for the Business of Government.

Gronlund, A., & Horan, T. (2005). Introducing e-gov: History, definitions and issues. *Communications of the Association for Information Systems, 15*, 713–729.

Heeks, R., & Bailur, S. (2007). Analyzing e-government research: Perspectives, philosophies, theories, methods, and practice. *Government Information Quarterly, 24*, 243–265.

Hirschheim, R., & Smithson, S. (1999). Evaluation of information systems: A critical assessment. In L. Willcocks, & S. Lester (Eds.), *Beyond the IT productivity paradox West Sussex* (pp. 381–409). New York: Wiley.

ICT Compendium. (2007). Retrieved July 27, 2015, from http://unpan1.un.org/intradoc/groups/public/documents/un/unpan030003.pdf

Innovative practices that won the UNPSA, please see iPad/iPhone application that we developed: UN Innovations in Public Governance, http://itunes.apple.com/us/app/un-innovations-in-public-governance/id443218537?mt=8

Irani, Z. (2000). Critical evaluation and integration of information systems. *Business Process Management Journal, 8*(4), 314–317.

Irani, Z., & Love, P. (2001). The propagation of technology management taxonomies for evaluating investments in information systems. *Journal of Management Information Systems, 17*(3), 161–177.

Irani, Z., Love, P., & Montazemi, A. (2006). Call for papers: Special issue on egovernment: Past, present and future. *European Journal of Information Systems, 16*(2), 155–164.

Isidore, C. (2011). America's lost trillions. *CNN Money*. 9 June 2011. Web. November, 11 2015. http://money.cnn.com/2011/06/09/news/economy/household_wealth/

Jamali, D. (2004). Success and failure mechanisms of public private partnerships (PPPs) in developing countries: Insights from the Lebanese context. *International Journal of Public Sector Management, 17*(5), 414–430.

Jeong, K., & Kim, H. (2003). After the introduction of the government portal services: Evolution into the m-government initiatives. *Proceedings of the ICA 37th conference*, Barcelona

Jones, S., Irani, Z., & Sharif, A. (2007). E-government evaluation: Reflections on three organizational case studies. *Proceedings of the 40th Hawaii international conference on system sciences* (pp. 1–8). IEEE.

Kauzya, J. (2010). *Repositioning the African public services for the realization of national visions topic: Enhancing public administration effectiveness in Africa through strengthening local leadership capacity*. 32nd AAPAM annual roundtable conference. Durban, November 15–19, 2010. Paper presentation.

Kim, H., Pan, G., & Pan, S. (2007). Managing IT-enabled transformation in the public sector: A case study on e-government in South Korea. *Government Information Quarterly, 24*, 338–352.

Kushchu, I., & Kuscu, H. (2003). *From E-government to M-government: Facing the Inevitable*. The 3rd European conference on e-government.

Lessig, L. (2011). *Republic, lost: How money corrupts Congress—and a plan to stop it*. New York: Twelve. Print.

Liu, S., & Yuan, Q. (2015). The evolution of information and communication technology in public administration. *Public Administration and Development, 35*(2), 140–151.

Mackintosh, A. (1988). Dr. Atanasoff's computer. *Scientific American, 259*(2), 90–96.

Markendahl, J., Östen, M., & Werding, J. (2009). Business innovation strategies to reduce the revenue gap for wireless broadband services. *Communications and Strategies, 75*(3), 35.

Measuring the Information Society. (2011). Retrieved July 27, 2015, from http://www.itu.int/ITU-D/ict/publications/idi/2011/index.html

Morris, D. F., & Moon, M. J. (2005). Advancing e-government at the grassroots: Tortoise or hare? *Public Administration Review, 65*(1), 64–75.

Mulgan, R. (2000). Accountability: An ever-expanding concept? *Public Administration, 78*(3), 55–73.

National Patient Summary. (2012). http://www.epractice.eu/en/news/5347051

Northrup, T. A., & Thorson, S. J. (2003). The Web of governance and democratic accountability. *Proceedings of the 36th annual Hawaii international conference on system sciences*, Hawaii.

OECD. ITU publication-MDGs data, http://www.un.org/millenniumgoals/stats.shtml

OECD/International Telecommunication Union. (2011). M-Government Mobile Technologies for Responsive Governments and Connected Societies. Retrieved July 26, 2015, from http://www.oecd-ilibrary.org/governance/m-government-mobile-technologies-for-responsive-governments-and-connected-societies_9789264118706-en

Ostberg, O. A. (2003). Swedish view on mobile government. *Proceedings of international symposium on E- & M-government*, London.

Premkumar, G., Ho, A., & Chakraborty, P. (2006). E-government evolution: An evaluation of local online services. *IJEB International Journal of Electronic Business, 4*, 177–177.

Reddick, C. (2005). Citizen interaction with e-government: From the streets to servers? *Government Information Quaterly, 22*, 38–57.

Reddick, C., & Turner, M. (2012). Channel choice and public service delivery in Canada: Comparing e-government to traditional service delivery. *Government Information Quarterly, 29*(1), 1–11.

Relyea, H. C., & Hogue, H. B. (2004). A brief history of the emergence of digital government in the United States. In A. Pavlichev & G. D. Garson (Eds.), *Digital government: Principles and best practices* (pp. 16–33). Hershey, PA: Idea Group Publishing.

Remenyi, D., & Money, A. (2000). *The effective measurement and management of IT costs and benefits* (2nd ed.). Oxford: Butterworth-Heinemann.

Rotman, D. (2013). Biotech crops will have an essential role in ensuring that there's enough to eat. *MIT Technology Review.* December 17, 2013. Web. July 27, 2015. http://www.technologyreview.com/featuredstory/522596/why-we-will-need-genetically-modified-foods/

Seifert, J. W., & Relyea, H. C. (2004). Considering e-government from the federal perspective: An evolving concept, a developing practice. *Journal of E-Government, 1*(1), 7–15.

Seifter, J. & Chung, J. (2008). Using e-government to reinforce government-citizen relationships. *Social Science Computer Reviews, 27*, 3–23.

Shi, Y. (2007). The accessibility of Chinese local government websites: An exploratory study. *Government Information Quarterly, 24*(2), 377–403.

Song, G. (2005). Transcending e-government: A case of mobile government in Beijing. *The first European conference on mobile government.* Sussex. July 2005.

Streib, G., & Navarro, I. (2006). Citizen demand for interactive e-government: The case of georgia consumer services. *American Review of Public Administration, 36*(3), 288–300.

The Annual Report. (2007). "The user challenge – Benchmarking the supply of online public services" prepared for the European Commission. Directorate General for Information Society and Media, September 2007.

The Economist. (2008, February 7). The limits of leapfrogging: The spread of new technologies often depends on the availability of older ones. Retrieved November 11, 2015, From http://www.economist.com/node/10650775

The Limits of Leapfrogging. (2008, February 9). *The economist.* Retrieved July 26, 2015.

The Report for Congress. A primer on e-government, 2003 mentions four stages.

The Transformation of Government. World economic forum. Retrieved July 27, 2015, from http://www.weforum.org/news/future-government-lessons-learned-around-world

Thede, N. (2009). Decentralization, democracy and human rights: A human rights-based analysis of the impact of local democratic reforms on development. *Journal of Human Development and Capabilities, 10*(1), 103–123.

Tian, J., & Tianfield, H. (2003). Some perspectives of e-government. In F. Bannister, & D. Remenyi (Eds.), *3rd European conference on e-government.*

Timmons, H. (2008). In a season of discontent, many protests sweep India. *The New York Times*. 29 Jun. 2008. Web. Retrieved November 11, 2015, from http://www.nytimes.com/2008/06/29/world/asia/29india.html

Trimi, S., & Sheng, H. (2008). Emerging trends in m-governement. *Communications of the ACM, 51*(5), 53–58.

UN Department of Economic and Social Affairs. (2012). United Nations e-government survey 2012: E-Government for the people. Retrieved from http://unpan3.un.org/egovkb/global_reports/12report.htm

UN Public Service Awards. (2013). Governments have to use innovative means to deliver public services. Retrieved from http://www.un.org/en/development/desa/news/administration/public-services.html

United Nations Global. *E-Government Readiness Report 2005 mentions five stages*, p. 16.

United Nations Millennium Goals. (2005). http://www.un.org/millenniumgoals/bkgd.shtml

Unlocking the Human Potential for Public Sector Performance. (2005). United Nations. Department of Economic and Social Affairs.

UNPSA nominees. http://www.unpan.org/DPADM/UNPSDayAwards/KnowledgeBaseofUNPublicServiceAwards/tabid/1260/language/en-US/Default.aspx

Van de Ven, A. (1986). Central problems in the management of innovation. *Management Science, 32*, 590–607.

Velsen, L., Geest, T., Hedde, M., & Derks, W. (2009). Requirements engineering for e-government services: A citizen-centric approach and case study. *Government Information Quarterly, 26*, 477–486.

Willcocks, L., & Lester, S. (1999). Information technology: Transformer or sink hole. In L. Willcocks & S. Lester (Eds.), *Beyond the IT productivity paradox* (pp. 1–36). West Sussex: Wiley.

World Bank. Definition of e-government. http://go.worldbank.org/M1JHE0Z280

World Bank. Why We Should Care About Inequality. (2012, March 30). Retrieved from http://web.worldbank.org/WBSITE/EXTERNAL/TOPICS/EXTPOVERTY/0,,contentMDK:23157030~pagePK:210058~piPK:210062~theSitePK:336992,00.html

World Summit Awards in E-Government Content/App. http://www.wsis-award.org/winners/e-government-and-institutions

MIX
Papier aus verantwortungsvollen Quellen
Paper from responsible sources
FSC® C105338

If you have any concerns about our products,
you can contact us on
ProductSafety@springernature.com

In case Publisher is established outside the EU,
the EU authorized representative is:
Springer Nature Customer Service Center GmbH
Europaplatz 3, 69115 Heidelberg, Germany

Printed by Libri Plureos GmbH
in Hamburg, Germany